Dangerous Exits

Critical Issues in Crime and Society

Raymond J. Michalowski, Series Editor

Tammy L. Anderson, ed., *Neither Villain Nor Victim: Empowerment and Agency among Women Substance Abusers*

Mary Bosworth and Jeanne Flavin, eds., *Race, Gender, and Punishment: From Colonialism to the War on Terror*

Loretta Capeheart and Dragan Milovanovic, *Social Justice: Theories, Issues, and Movements*

Patricia E. Erickson and Steven K. Erickson, *Crime, Punishment, and Mental Illness: Law and the Behavioral Sciences in Conflict*

Luis A. Fernandez, *Policing Dissent: Social Control and the Anti-Globalization Movement*

Michael J. Lynch, *Big Prisons, Big Dreams: Crime and the Failure of America's Penal System*

Raymond J. Michalowski and Ronald C. Kramer, eds., *State-Corporate Crime: Wrongdoing at the Intersection of Business and Government*

Susan L. Miller, *Victims as Offenders: The Paradox of Women's Violence in Relationships*

Anthony M. Platt, *The Child Savers: The Invention of Delinquency*, 40th Anniversary Edition with an introduction and critical commentaries compiled by Miroslava Chávez-García

Susan F. Sharp, *Hidden Victims: The Effects of the Death Penalty on Families of the Accused*

Robert H. Tillman and Michael L. Indergaard, *Pump and Dump: The Rancid Rules of the New Economy*

Mariana Valverde, *Law and Order: Images, Meanings, Myths*

Michael Welch, *Crimes of Power & States of Impunity: The U.S. Response to Terror*

Michael Welch, *Scapegoats of September 11th: Hate Crimes and State Crimes in the War on Terror*

Dangerous Exits

Escaping Abusive
Relationships
in Rural America

Walter S. DeKeseredy
and
Martin D. Schwartz

Rutgers University Press
New Brunswick, New Jersey, and London

LIBRARY OF CONGRESS CATALOGING-IN-PUBLICATION DATA

DeKeseredy, Walter S., 1959–
    Dangerous exits : escaping abusive relationships in rural America /
Walter S. DeKeseredy, Martin D. Schwartz.
        p.   cm. — (Critical issues in crime and society)
    Includes bibliographical references and index.
    ISBN 978-0-8135-4518-9 (hardcover : alk. paper) —
ISBN 978-0-8135-4519-6 (pbk. : alk. paper)
    1. Wife abuse—Ohio—Case studies.   2. Sexual abuse victims—Ohio—
Case studies.   3. Sociology, Rural—Ohio—Case studies.   4. Patriarchy—
Ohio—Case studies.   I. Schwartz, Martin D.   II. Title.
    HV6626.22.O35D445 2009
    362.82'9209771091734—dc22   2008035433

A British Cataloging-in-Publication record for this book is available
from the British Library.

Visit our Web site: http://rutgerspress.rutgers.edu

Manufactured in the United States of America
Typesetting: BookType

Contents

Foreword by Joseph F. Donnermeyer   vii
Preface   xi
Acknowledgments   xiii

1. *Introduction: The Dark Side of the Heartland*   1

2. *Thinking Theoretically about Separation
and Divorce Sexual Assault*   27

3. *The Study: Doing Feminist Research
in the Heartland*   47

4. *Exiting Dangerous Relationships: Rural Women's
Experiences of Abuse and Risk Factors*   61

5. *The Consequences of Abuse and Women's
Social Support Experiences*   81

6. *Where Do We Go from Here? Research,
Theory, and Policy*   96

Appendix A.
Separation/Divorce Sexual Assault Screen Questions   127
Appendix B.
Semi-Structured Interview Schedule   131
Notes   137
References   143
Index   161

FOREWORD

Dangerous Exits speaks to the plight of rural women (and women everywhere) in abusive relationships. Walter DeKeseredy and Martin Schwartz vividly describe the ways in which rural culture and rural society (and culture and society everywhere) can enable these forms of violence to both emerge and persist. Further, this work passionately advocates for ways that rural communities (and all places, everywhere) can and should respond to a social problem covered up by layers of traditional and anachronistic assumptions about the roles of women and men in society, by the skewed and biased responses (and often, no response) of some rural law enforcement and social agencies serving rural populations, and by norms of tolerance (and even silence) among neighbors, kin, clergy, and local leaders for behaviors that should produce moral outrage.

Dangerous Exits is so multidimensional in its approach that it simultaneously informs the literature in rural criminology, critical criminology, feminist criminology, feminist studies in general, police studies, the sociology of the community, social action and community development, rural sociology, violence against women, and the treatment and rehabilitation of crime victims. However, it is not simply the number of diverse ways that the reader can approach this book that makes it a significant contribution to the literature. It is the incredible number of lessons contained within the stories of forty-three rural women, combined with the scholarship of DeKeseredy and Schwartz.

The authors point out that violence against women is a form of terrorism invisible to most of the public, hidden behind a silent wall of women too intimidated and fearful to act, communities in denial about problems that exist in their own backyards, and criminal justice and social service agencies who seem to have other priorities.

Weaving quotations from the forty-three rural women they interviewed with literature from criminology, feminist studies, and rural sociology, DeKeseredy and Schwartz demonstrate why a critical perspective should be a primary approach to the study of rural crime in the years ahead. While many scholars of rural sociology have taken an approach to research and theorizing that reflects the observation of C. W. Mills that personal troubles must be understood within the context of public issues, most rural sociologists do not consciously embrace a critical perspective. This is probably because most rural sociologists feel compelled to approach their work seeking a multilevel sociological understanding of rural issues, which recognizes that what happens at specific rural and remote places, and to the people who live there, cannot be understood without reference to social structures, social change, and relationships of dependency with the larger world, especially when economic, political, and cultural power resides mostly at urban centers.

DeKeseredy and Schwartz see things that many other scholars do not. For example, they inform readers, rural communities are as diverse as cities and suburbs, and simplistic rural-urban dichotomies are not very good ways to approach the study of rural crime in general, and of separation and divorce sexual assault specifically.

Perhaps of greater importance, by linking social structure and culture as expressed in the rural context, the authors pose a tough, scholarly challenge to mainstream criminological theory and related research, especially that associated with social disorganization theory and its revision around the concept of collective efficacy. The authors also challenge rural sociologists who have uncritically grabbed hold of the concept of social capital as if it always functions for the good of rural people. As DeKeseredy and Schwartz illustrate, crime in all its dimensions varies according to what kinds of social organization, forms of collective efficacy, and expressions of social capital are in play. For example, as many of the women in this book attest from experience, men in the rural context described here support and encourage their peers to abuse women. To show how some rural men learn, act out, and obtain approval for their abusing and violent behavior by peers, the authors describe relationships and primary group networks that fall within what many criminologists and rural sociologists refer to as gemeinschaft.

Dangerous Exits never lets us forget that nonintervention and minimal assistance on the part of family, friends, neighbors, and law enforcement represent the norm in many local, rural social structures. And, the authors show, these enablers of violence against rural women exist alongside the very features of rural places that constrain violence, abusive actions, and for that matter, all forms of crime. Along with the mistaken idea of a straightforward rural-urban dichotomy, which fails to appreciate the diversity of rural places, we must also discard the hackneyed notion that organization means less crime and that disorganization means more crime. It is not that simple.

In terms of the new scholarship on rural crime, this book deserves a special place. First, DeKeseredy and Schwartz revise their own model, reevaluating their and others' naïve views about rural communities and the ways in which traditional criminological approaches fail to appreciate the connection between rural social structure, culture, and crime.

Second, the authors ask their interviewees for their own recommendations for change. Familiar recommendations for better educational and job opportunities, subsidized housing, greater awareness of the problem in society and local communities, and so on take on fresh meaning in these women's words, unaffected by academic jargon. These are real people, with real problems, telling us what they need to improve their own lives, to stop the abuse, and to change local communities and local cultures so that they constrain, not enable, the problem.

Finally, building upon and reinforcing the recommendations of their subjects, DeKeseredy and Schwartz lay out an agenda for improving the situation of rural survivors of separation and divorce sexual assault, "modest proposals" that together comprise a powerful call for action and policy change.

The content and context of violence against rural women forms the core of *Dangerous Exits*, with accounts of abusive and violent behavior related by the victims themselves. The book ultimately is a straightforward description of the mental, physical, economic, and social costs to rural survivors of separation and divorce sexual assault. It is a frank account of victims who fight the odds to find a road to recovery that does not double back to the same place and to the same situation, and who do not always succeed.

I invite you to read and explore Dangerous Exits, both for what it says about a real, serious, and mostly invisible rural social problem, and as a monograph destined to become a classic piece of scholarship that did much to advance the study of rural criminology.

Joseph F. Donnermeyer, Professor
Rural Sociology
The Ohio State University

PREFACE

Since the 1970s, social scientists have greatly enhanced an empirical and theoretical understanding of various types of woman abuse in ongoing heterosexual relationships, such as dating, cohabitation, and marriage. Still, although we know that breaking up with a patriarchal and/or abusive man is one of the most dangerous events in a woman's life, relatively little attention has thus far been paid to the victimization of women who want to leave, are in the process of leaving, or who have left their marital or cohabiting partners. Further, the limited work done on this topic focuses primarily on homicide and nonlethal variants of male physical violence. Woman abuse, of course, is multidimensional in nature and a few U.S. studies show that many women are also at high risk of being sexually assaulted during and after separation or divorce. Nevertheless, almost all the research on this problem, regardless of whether it is qualitative or quantitative, was done in urban areas, such as Boston and San Francisco.

The main objective of this book, then, is to help fill a major research gap by presenting the results of a qualitative study of separation and divorce sexual assault in three rural Ohio communities. Guided by previous relevant research and an integrated theory constructed by Walter S. DeKeseredy, McKenzie Rogness, and Martin D. Schwartz, this project was funded by National Institute of Justice Grant 2002-WG-BX-0004 and involved interviewing forty-three rural Ohio women who experienced considerable pain and suffering as the result of separation and divorce sexual assault and other forms of abuse. The data gathered from these women are, to the best of our knowledge, the very first of their kind and seriously challenge the commonly held notion of rural communities as immune from high levels of woman abuse.

One of the key risk factors identified in our study and given much attention in this book is male peer support, which is defined by Walter

DeKeseredy as "attachments to male peers and the resources they provide which encourage and legitimate woman abuse." Except for Neil Websdale's Kentucky study described in his 1998 book *Rural Woman Battering and the Justice System: An Ethnography*, no prior empirical attempt has been made to understand the nature and content of pro-abuse male social networks in rural U.S. communities. Most male peer support research, including our own, has been quantitative in nature and limited to explaining woman abuse on college campuses. Moreover, no other study has concentrated on whether male peer support contributes to sexual assault either during or after the termination of an intimate relationship.

In addition to focusing on how male peer support is strongly associated with separation and divorce sexual assault, *Dangerous Exits* addresses the influence of other major determinants of such assault, such as pornography, men's adherence to the ideology of familial patriarchy, men's patterns of alcohol and drug consumption, and the absence of effective informal and formal measures of social control. The consequences of the abuse our respondents experienced are also described, as well as their policy recommendations. We offer our own progressive policy proposals in chapter 6.

Acknowledgments

In addition to receiving funds to conduct the study reported in this book from the National Institute of Justice, Walter DeKeseredy obtained financial assistance from the College of Arts and Sciences and the Office of the Vice President of Research at Ohio University. Arguments and findings included in this book are ours and do not represent the official position of the U.S. Department of Justice or Ohio University.

The study described in this book could not have been done without the participation of the forty-three rural Ohio women who took the time and effort to reveal their terrifying experiences to us. We will always remember their courage, strength, and support. We hope the results of our project will help improve their safety and well-being and contribute to the creation of effective policies aimed at curbing the many harms uncovered by our research.

Walter DeKeseredy's National Institute of Justice (NIJ) grant monitors, Katharine Darke and Leora Rosen, were strong sources of support and guidance. Others affiliated with NIJ's Violence and Victimization Division also provided us with much encouragement and valuable advice, including Bernie Auchter, Karen Bachar, Catherine McNamee, Angela Moore, and Marge Zahn.

Certainly, our book is the product of a collective effort, and obviously, we wrote it with the assistance offered by many men and women heavily involved in the ongoing and ever-changing struggle to end woman abuse. People affiliated with the Ohio Domestic Violence Network, the Athens County Coalition Against Sexual Assault, the Ohio Coalition Against Sexual Assault, various social services based in Athens and other parts of rural Ohio, the California Coalition Against Sexual Assault, and other organizations played a key role in the developmental and data-gathering phases of our study. Many thanks also go to Walter DeKeseredy's energetic and deeply committed research assistants Megan Cameron, Jessica Edgar, Danielle Fagen, Mandy Hall, Carolyn Joseph, and McKenzie Rogness. While Dr. Judith Grant of the University of Ontario Institute of Technology was affiliated with Ohio University, she helped the research team come into contact with abuse survivors and made many other important contributions to various stages of the study, including patiently waiting for calls from potential interviewees and helping train the research team.

The seeds of research reported in this book were actually sown in discussions Walter DeKeseredy held with Raquel Kennedy Bergen, Mary Koss, Claire M. Renzetti, and Karen Bachar. Walter hopes one day to team up with these close friends and colleagues to conduct the study they originally planned to do. Joseph F. Donnermeyer also played an instrumental role in the development and completion of this book. His help went, as it always does, beyond the call of duty. For example, he sensitized us to many important publications on rural criminology and rural sociology that we cite throughout *Dangerous Exits*. On top of helping us enhance our knowledge of rural social scientific research, Joe took much time away from his busy schedule to exchange ideas about topics addressed in each chapter and was gracious enough to write the foreword to our book.

In addition to receiving considerable help from all these people, we have greatly benefited from the comments, criticisms, lessons, and influences provided by the following friends and colleagues: Shahid Alvi, Nawal Ammar, Ashley Bannon, Victoria Banyard, Gregg Barak, Rebecca Block, Susan Caringella, Meda Chesney-Lind, Molly Dragiewicz, Marc Dubin, Chrissie Eith, William F. Flack Jr., Jennifer Gibbs, Alberto Godenzi, Barbara Hart, Sally Laskey, Susan L. Miller, Stephen L. Muzzatti, Patrik Olsson, Barbara Perry, Ruth Peterson, Gary Potter, Aysan Sev'er, Susan F. Sharp, Kenneth D. Tunnell, and Neil Websdale.

Of course, *Dangerous Exits* came to fruition with the encouragement and help of our Rutgers University Press editor Adi Hovav; of our copy editor, Bobbe Needham; and of Raymond J. Michalowski Jr., who is the editor of Rutgers University Press's Critical Issues in Crime and Society Series. Adi and Ray, we can't thank you enough for all you have done for us. Also, words cannot possibly describe our gratitude to our loved ones. We are especially indebted to Carol Blum, Pat, Andrea, Ola, and Steven

DeKeseredy, and to Eva Jantz. Their inexhaustible support helped us maintain our energy and focus, although it sometimes drained theirs.

This book includes material adapted from Walter S. DeKeseredy (2007), *Sexual Assault during and after Separation/Divorce: An Exploratory Study* (report prepared for the U.S. Department of Justice); Walter S. DeKeseredy, Shahid Alvi, Claire M. Renzetti, and Martin D. Schwartz (2004), "Reducing Private Violence against Women in Public Housing: Can Second-Generation CPTED Make a Difference?" (*CPTED Journal* 3:27–36); Walter S. DeKeseredy, Joseph F. Donnermeyer, and Martin D. Schwartz (forthcoming), "Preventing Woman Abuse in Rural Communities: The Contribution of a Gendered Second-Generation CPTED" (*Security Journal*); Walter S. DeKeseredy, Joseph F. Donnermeyer, Martin D. Schwartz, Kenneth D. Tunnell, and Mandy Hall (2007), "Thinking Critically about Rural Gender Relations: Toward a Rural Masculinity Crisis/ Male Peer Support Model of Separation/Divorce Sexual Assault" (*Critical Criminology* 15:295–311); Walter S. DeKeseredy and Carolyn Joseph (2006), "Separation/Divorce Sexual Assault in Rural Ohio: Preliminary Results of an Exploratory Study" (*Violence against Women* 12:301–311); Walter S. DeKeseredy, McKenzie Rogness, and Martin D. Schwartz (2004), "Separation/Divorce Sexual Assault: The Current State of Social Scientific Knowledge" (*Aggression and Violent Behavior* 9:675–691); and Walter S. DeKeseredy, Martin D. Schwartz, Danielle Fagen, and Mandy Hall (2006), "Separation/Divorce Sexual Assault: The Contribution of Male Peer Support" (*Feminist Criminology* 1:228–250).

Dangerous Exits

CHAPTER 1

Introduction

THE DARK SIDE OF THE HEARTLAND

It's like we see, but we don't. It's like three monkeys:
don't see, don't hear, don't speak.

—Jackie, rural Ohio interviewee

IN EARLY JUNE 2008, as we finished this book, U.S. senators Hillary Clinton and Barak Obama were energetically competing for the Democratic presidential nomination. Not surprisingly, journalists repeatedly asked them pointed questions about their positions on the war in Iraq. They also frequently queried Republican presidential candidate Senator John McCain about his stand on this controversial war. As we appreciate the sacrifice of the many U.S. troops who have been killed and injured serving their country in Iraq, a war not likely to end soon, let us not forget the plight of U.S. soldiers fighting in Afghanistan. "Hostiles" in both countries have killed close to three thousand U.S. troops, and "non-hostiles" have killed about eight hundred (Vallee 2007). The constant media attention is therefore justified, and so are heated public debates among politicians, academics, and the public.

As you read this book, many young Americans stationed overseas are trying to outmaneuver enemy forces, stay one step ahead of them, protect innocent people, and stay alive for another day. They are heroes and warrant much respect for being in harm's way. It seems, though, that the bulk of U.S. citizens forget, ignore, or are unaware of victims of another war, one that has gone on for at least three thousand years (Cross 2007). Certainly, the same can be said about citizens or residents of most other countries. Right now, "in numbers that would numb the mind of

Einstein," thousands of women in the United States are experiencing great physical, psychological, and economic pain (Stephen Lewis cited in Vallee 2007, 22).[1] For them, the enemies are not international terrorists, insurgents, or psychotic predatory strangers. Rather, the enemies are "intimate terrorists" (M. Johnson 2008). They are men with whom these women are experiencing, have experienced, or want to establish a sexual and/or emotional relationship. If the death toll in Afghanistan and Iraq is an unsettling truth, so is the alarming amount of woman abuse that occurs behind closed doors in every U.S. community.

For example, contrary to popular belief, sexual assault on college campuses is commonplace. Large- and small-scale surveys consistently show that approximately 25 percent of female undergraduates experience some variation of this crime every year. Nevertheless, many faculty, administrators, and students trivialize or ignore sexual assaults on campus. Such a response is ironic given the current discussions on and reactions to crime, often characterized by frequent calls for more aid to victims, more prisons and longer sentences, and more death sentences.

A burglary or robbery rate of 25 percent would turn a college campus upside down, but some believe that when the crime is sexual victimization of women, there is less concern. There are many reasons for this, but the most important, say some experts, are gender politics and powerful interest groups with stakes in denying the extent of sexual assaults on college campuses. For example, some "new generation feminists" like Katie Roiphe (1993) and conservative academics such as Neil Gilbert (1991) and John Fekete (1994) assert that the high rates of sexual assault reported in refereed academic journals and scholarly books greatly exaggerate the case. For these people, there is no serious problem of rape on college campuses; rather there is a "phantom epidemic" produced by "pseudoscientific" studies guided by feminist stereotypes.

A case in point. In March 2006, Walter DeKeseredy and psychologist William F. Flack Jr. met with a lawyer at a small private U.S. university to discuss sexual assault on his campus and its immediate surroundings. He stated that a recent study of unwanted sex at his school is flawed and at best reveals a high rate of "regretted sex." When DeKeseredy told him that unless his university developed an effective prevention plan, there was a strong likelihood that victims' parents would sue, this lawyer replied that he was more worried about lawsuits filed by "alleged perpetrators." Such a concern presumes that false allegations of sexual assault are more signif-icant problems than true ones. However, less than 2 percent of campus rapes reported to the police prove to involve false allegations by the victims (Bohmer and Parrot 1993; DeKeseredy and Flack 2007).

Further evidence of what journalist Brian Vallee (2007) refers to as a "war on women" is that annually at least 11 percent of North American women in marital/cohabiting relationships are physically abused by their male partners (DeKeseredy, Ellis, and Alvi 2005). Unfortunately, crime prevention advice fails to take this information into account. Women are commonly warned about the dangers of living and traveling alone and the need to avoid unlit areas, but they are rarely told that the place they are most likely to be victimized is at home by their intimate partners. Further, they are frequently advised to break up such relationships when they turn violent, a move that could actually put them at greater risk, which is one of the key points we make in this book.

Still, to this day, when we discuss our work on male-to-female violence with people who lack expertise on this problem, we are often asked, "Why don't battered women just leave home?" We also frequently hear, "If it happened to me, I'd be out the door in a flash." The truth is that the overwhelming majority of women *do* leave, but there are many reasons why a woman might choose to stay in an abusive relationship. Some women are simply afraid to leave—often with excellent reason. They have become convinced that they will be beaten if they stay but killed if they try to leave. After living with abusive men for years, they are often much better judges than we of what the men are capable of doing. Other women are afraid of being on their own. This may be an economic issue; they do not believe they can house and feed their children. It may be a problem of self-esteem; after years of being belittled, they have come to believe that they are not capable of making decisions for themselves. Generally, however, attempts to study battered women to see how they are "different" (low self-esteem, low intelligence, fewer economic resources, a history of violence in the family, personality differences) are rarely fruitful. Battered women are just like any other women, except that they are caught in a situation of frightening proportions. In fact, the domestic war described in this book could overtake any woman (LaViolette and Barnett 2000).

Death goes hand and hand with any violent war, and the one of central concern in this book is no exception. It is estimated that in the

United States, intimate partners kill 1,200 to 1,300 women every year (Vallee 2007, 30). Is it not time, then, for us to wake up? Violence against women is neither rare nor greatly exaggerated by feminist academics, activists, and practitioners with an axe to grind. It is all around us. It is a global problem that damages our public health—many commentators assert that U.S. intimate relationships and institutions are experiencing an "epidemic" of woman abuse. Actually, the term is out of place here. To health officials, an epidemic is a disease that devastates a population and eventually subsides. Male-to-female physical, sexual, psychological, and other forms of violence, however, seem to be deeply entrenched in the U.S. population. Thus, if we term woman abuse a disease, it is in its endemic phase (DeKeseredy, Schwartz, and Alvi 2000), possibly comparable to hard drug use among disadvantaged North American inner-city residents (Currie 1993).

Unfortunately, medical treatment will not cure violence against women. Although the biological and psychological consequences of such victimization may require medical attention, data presented in this book show that woman abuse is a social problem that can be curbed only through the creation and implementation of policies that target the broader social and social psychological forces that perpetuate and legitimate intimate violence.

This is not to say that woman abuse has been totally ignored in recent decades. For example, since the 1980s, we have seen:

Increased awareness and more education programs;

police training programs concerning woman abuse;

police affirmative action hiring programs to increase the number of women officers;

mandatory arrest policies;

a major increase in the number of shelters for battered women;

the creation of domestic violence courts;

the creation of the Violence against Women Act;

a growth in batterers' treatment programs;

resources and services for children who have witnessed woman abuse; and

coordinated, community-based approaches.

On the surface these changes and other policies, laws, and initiatives aimed at curbing rape, wife beating, stalking, and the like look promising and effective. Still, some of them mirror the factors that create woman abuse and do not target the broader social, political, and economic forces that contribute to this harm. For example, harsh law-and-order approaches silence many abused women, because they cannot tell their story in a traditional justice setting and have their worth reconfirmed. Moreover, in cases where the battered women syndrome is the defense, courts tend to see psychiatrists as the only credible expert witnesses, thus reinforcing the idea that woman abuse is a medical or psychiatric problem. Then, of course, increasingly, women who seek help for abuse-related mental health issues find their help-seeking behavior used against them in child custody and access cases (Dragiewicz and DeKeseredy 2008).

We could easily provide a much longer list of problems and challenges abused women now face, but the main point to consider here is that policy decisions can have profound effects on the ways people relate to a life experience and act on it. Looking at the problem of woman abuse by tracing policy decisions generates considerable unease. While awareness and concern about the prevalence of various types of woman abuse have grown substantially over the past few decades, and while governments and organizations have put millions of dollars and many hours into attempts to reduce abuse, some of the policies put into place to curb this problem often thwart their own apparent aim (DeKeseredy and MacLeod 1997; Jaffe, Lemon, and Poisson 2003).

In sum, abused women now have more resources to choose from, but there is still a war on against them and they are not markedly safer. Further, while empirical and theoretical work on male-to-female abuse has grown dramatically in the last thirty-five years, relatively little of this has focused on the victimization of rural women in the United States, especially those who want to leave, are trying to leave, are in the process of leaving, or who have left their male partners. Thus, based on a study conducted in rural Ohio, a key objective of this book is to give voice to a marginalized group of women who, for the most part, have suffered in silence. We could not agree more with Gregg Barak (2007, 89), who asserts that "academics and policy makers alike . . . often focus too exclusively on the urban environment to the detriment of the rural environment, as well as on the plight of the minority of battered women who stay rather than the majority of battered and unbattered women who leave and who ultimately appear to be subject to even a greater danger or higher level of violence than those who stay."

CRIMINOLOGY AND THE FALSE IMAGES OF RURAL LIFE

Rural crime, including male assaults on women, has ranked among the least studied social problems in criminology (DeKeseredy, Donnermeyer, Schwartz, Tunnell, and Hall 2007). As Donnermeyer, Jobes, and Barclay (2006, 199) put it in their comprehensive review of rural crime research: "If rural crime was considered at all, it was a convenient 'ideal type' contrasted with the criminogenic conditions assumed to exist exclusively in urban locations. Rural crime was rarely examined, either comparatively with urban crime or as a subject worthy of investigation in its own right." This book, then, tells a different story about rural communities from the one usually told by criminologists and the media, who rarely give voice to the female survivors of domestic violence; again, our goal is to address this selective inattention.

Common images in fictional and nonfictional accounts of rural life portray a slower, more peaceful way of life, picturesque farms, Main Street businesses that give personal service to long-standing customers, little schoolhouses with dedicated teachers and studious pupils, and a sheriff who knows everyone by their first name (Hay and Basran 1992). Further, newspapers and other media often characterize rural people as being nicer to each other than urban residents are (Toughill 2007). Of course, the media also often portray rural communities as remaining "somewhat behind the times" (Gray 2007).

But the mass media's picture of the rural-urban divide is frequently inaccurate. For example, contrary to what many people claim, data presented in this book and elsewhere show that rural people are not necessarily more likely to help people they know, including relatives, neighbors, or friends (DeKeseredy, Donnermeyer, et al. 2007; Statistics Canada 2005). Our data also challenge myths about "rural warmth and hospitality" perpetuated by some journalists and others who perceive "small-town folks to be nicer" (Toughill 2007; Turcotte 2005). In fact, many, if not most, rural people are very suspicious of "outsiders" (DeKeseredy 2007b; Zorza 2002).

Mass media may also emphasize tight-knit communities, strong family ties, and rugged individualism in rural areas (Frank 2003), as S. Robert Lichter, Daniel Amundson, and Linda Lichter (2003, 1) note:

> There can be little doubt that American mass media have played a significant role in building and decorating these frames. From the late nineteenth-century dime novels that depicted the winning of the Wild West, to the "horse operas" that dominated the early days of television entertainment, to the big screen epics of John Wayne and John Huston, entertainment has idolized the rugged individual battling nature and human venality in the untamed west. More recent pop culture products like the television series *The Waltons* and *Little House on the Prairie*, along with cinematic hits like *Places in the Heart* and *The River* have presented warmer, more personal tales of rural Americans overcoming adversity and upholding traditional values. Even fluff like *Petticoat Junction, Green Acres*, and the *Dukes of Hazzard* have played a role in our collective associations with rural America.

Too, the media often play a key role in stereotyping as hillbillies the men who live in rural Appalachian areas like those in our study. Television shows such as *The Beverly Hillbillies*, some comic strips, and myriad joke books depict typical Appalachian men as "wearing the obligatory floppy hat, ragged shirt, and tattered baggy overalls" (Foster and Hummel 1997, 160). They are also frequently depicted as carrying muzzle-load rifles, sucking on corncob pipes, and drinking moonshine. They often have names like Clem, Zeke, or Jethro that imply they are illiterate (Williamson 1995). Sadly, such hillbilly caricatures encourage people to consider "southern mountaineers as backward, lazy, dumb, and unable to cope with the modern world" (Inge 1989, 915).

Most media stories about rural life prioritize men's experiences over those of women and rarely feature women as community leaders or family breadwinners. Rather such stories usually characterize rural women, especially those who live in Appalachia, as either hardened grandmothers or sexual objects (see box 1.1). There are exceptions, of course, including the role played by Jessica Lange in the 1984 film *Country*. In this movie, set within the context of the widespread foreclosures of farms in the early 1980s, Lange and actor Sam Shepard are married with children, and they and their neighbors face the threat of losing their farms.

Shepard loses hope and starts drinking, while Lange "remains strong and organizes the community to stand up for their land" (Oliver 2006, 1). Given that movies featuring strong women typically do not do well at the box office, it is not surprising that this one sold relatively few tickets even though it was critically acclaimed and Lange received her third Oscar nomination for her role as Jewell Ivy.

The Reality of Rural Life for Women

Popular films, documentaries, news stories, and TV shows may portray rural women as weak, unintelligent, seductive, or strong, but only rarely do they focus on male-to-female physical and sexual violence in rural communities. Even within criminology, studies do not give women like Jackie, quoted at the start of this chapter, the attention they need to help them lead safe, peaceful lives.[2] Jackie and many other rural women around the world daily experience much pain and suffering. Jackie is a survivor of sexual assault and other forms of woman abuse committed by a man she tried to leave. Although her case is not unique, many people believe that experiences like Jackie's are rare or isolated incidents. There are

---

1.1 Two Female Appalachian Caricatures

One is "Ma" or "Granny," a gaunt woman with straight, unkempt hair, often hidden by a large bonnet, wearing a tattered and patched dress and either high-topped work boots or no shoes at all. She is often portrayed as handy with a rifle, fond of a corncob pipe, and surrounded by her brood of "young'uns." Her face is wrinkled, and she is stooped from years of chopping wood and plowing, in contrast to the male who is depicted as snoozing, hunting, fishing, or making moonshine. In essence, this caricature is denied gender.

The other female caricature exploits gender and sexuality. She is scantily dressed in a halter-top and frayed denim short-shorts. Her waist is accentuated by curvaceous hips and an exaggerated bosom. Her legs are long, her lips are full, and she is barefoot, the inspiration for most of the women on Hee-Haw. She is named Daisy Mae or Lula Belle.

Source: Foster and Hummel 1997, 161.

several reasons for this belief, including the fact that rural male-to-female violence in intimate relationships is seldom reported to the police and when it is, these law enforcement officials often respond in ways described by another woman interviewed for the qualitative exploratory study that heavily informs this book: "Well, out here we deal with the Sheriff's Department outside the city limits. It would be nice if the deputies would stop rolling their eyeballs. You know, it's, uh, I don't think they treat domestic fights with enough seriousness. . . . I would like for the lawyers and the Sheriff's Department to be a little more sympathetic."

This response on the part of the legal system is not limited to rural areas. It is well known that many urban police officers ignore the plight of battered women and sexual assault survivors (Iovanni and Miller 2001). Still, while there is a system of social practices that generally dominates and oppresses rural and urban women alike, it operates differently in rural areas. For example, people in urban communities often complain of feeling anonymous, victims of an uncaring mysterious policing system. In rural communities, violent men are more likely to be protected by an "ol' boys network" (Websdale 1998). Certainly, many women know that the local police not only may be friends of their abusers, but also may refuse to arrest them on the grounds of this friendship (DeKeseredy and Joseph 2006; Zorza 2002).

Many people would claim that Jackie's experience is atypical because rural areas have higher levels of collective efficacy than do urban regions— that is, rural areas are characterized by what Sampson, Raudenbush, and Earls (1998, 1) refer to as "mutual trust among neighbors combined with a willingness to act on behalf of the common good, specifically to supervise children and maintain public order." This point is well taken, given that many rural people, including agents of social control such as police and judges, know each other socially, and rural areas are less tolerant of crime in general than are some metropolitan districts (Donnermeyer, Jobes, and Barclay 2006). But the point also just plain may not be true. Recent studies found some elements of the antithesis of collective efficacy—social disorganization—associated with arrest rates for juvenile violence in U.S. rural communities (Osgood and Chambers 2000, 2003).[3] Here, social disorganization is defined as "inability of a community structure to realize the common values of its residents and maintain effective controls" (Sampson and Groves 1989, 777).

To make matters more difficult, neither collective efficacy nor social disorganization may be operating according to a quiet textbook explanation. Collective efficacy in rural areas takes different shapes and forms and is not necessarily restricted to deterring or preventing crimes (Barclay, Donnermeyer, and Jobes 2004). Indeed, it may work in a way that increases the likelihood of violence, particularly against women. Moreover, what may appear to outsiders to be social disorganization is often "simply a different form of social organization if one takes the trouble to look closely" (Venkatesh 2000, 2006; Wacquant 1997, 346). Here is an account of how an all-male sexist network and other symptoms of what Websdale (1998) defines as "rural patriarchy" functioned to keep an Ohio woman we interviewed from leaving her abusive partner:

> Another time, after I finally got away from him and I was having these problems. I was, I was on drugs real heavy um, and I was trying to get away from him. He was still calling me. This was just in the last nine months. Um, I called Victim Awareness in my town and um, told them that I had been abused by him. Oh, they kept telling me that they was going to do something about it, and they never did. The one other time I went to Victim Awareness, they told me that um, they were going to question the neighbors and stuff. And the neighbors said that um, you know, they said that the neighbors didn't, didn't see or hear anything. So, they—I didn't have enough ah proof, so. Basically, nothing was ever done. He's a corrections officer in the town that I lived in, and he's friends with the sheriff and whoever else.

Another woman told us that the police officers who responded to several of her 911 calls were more empathetic toward the man who abused her than they were to her: "They have this whole attitude that they never give up, so that when they respond to a woman, they're apologizing to him as they lead him away." Similarly, Pam said, "Well, this is a rural area and all the cops know everybody and they're all family and they're very redneckish."

In sum, "social disorganization may facilitate some types of crime even as it constrains others" (Donnermeyer, Jobes, and Barclay 2006, 203). While rural residents may be able to count on their neighbors to help prevent public crimes such as vandalism, data we uncovered show that many rural men also rely on their male friends and neighbors, including those who are police officers, to support a violent patriarchal status quo, which these neighbors may interpret as acting on behalf of the common good. In rural sections of many states, widespread acceptance of woman abuse exists alongside related community norms that prohibit victims from publicly talking about their experiences and seeking social support (DeKeseredy and Joseph 2006; Krishnan, Hilbert, and Pase 2001; Lewis 2003). As mentioned earlier, the reactions of neighbors and other community members may be strong enough that we can say that they adhere to what Christopher Browning (2002) refers to as "nonintervention norms." This is what happened to Mary:

> There was too many of them that stood out of their homes and it was really aggravating, really aggravating when, I mean, it took my son to beg for my life. But here is our neighbors out here, seeing this man beat this female off the swing set, beating her with his fist, kicking her with his feet, grabbing her by the hair of her head, smearing her face and what, . . . you're gonna stand up there and aren't gonna call the law? Or you are gonna stand up there and you aren't gonna come down? Ya, we lived in the country. It was probably about, if you walked it, fifteen or twenty minutes up the hill before you got to their house. But they could clearly see us. And they was outside standing and he was just thumping me so hard, so hard. And nobody called the law. Nobody did. Nobody came down to yank him off me. Nobody did anything. But I had the pictures. I had the pictures of the bruises. The pictures of where he caught the house on fire. I had the pictures where he had the marks around my neck trying to kill me.

Other women told similar stories of the unwillingness of people in their community to help them. As one interviewee stated, "Nobody wants involved, honey." Another interviewee said essentially the same thing: "No, most of 'em didn't want to get involved." Moreover, some women, such as Mandy, experienced what Danielle Fagen (2005) refers to as a "community backlash" response to their victimization:

> I don't know what happened, really. That's why I'm doing a lot of reading, talking to people. I need to learn why this happened. Why did I get with him and not see it and everybody else around me saw it, you know, which even I lost two jobs being with him because

people don't want to get involved or they don't want to see that. And if you walk around with black and blue marks under your eyes, nobody wants to see that and they just judge you.

Many people assume that little crime occurs in rural U.S. communities, an assumption heavily fueled by the media, lay conversations, and even criminological research, which typically focuses on urban lawbreaking (Donnermeyer, Jobes, and Barclay 2006).[4] Similarly, many people view rural communities in Canada and Australia as safer than urban districts in those countries (Carrington 2007). According to newspaper reporter Theresa Boyle (2007): "After all, conventional wisdom holds that the big, bad city is the root of all evil. Small towns are supposed to be peaceful and serene." Certainly, "the characteristics of nostalgic fiction of yesterday are attributed to nonurban communities: they are a retreat from the brutalities of urban living, where people live closer to nature in simpler and (by implication) happier lives" (Campbell 2000, 562). Still, for Mary and other women we interviewed, nothing can be further from the truth. Their lives were a "living hell" when they tried to leave their male partners, and they received little, if any, social support.

Typically in the United States, and most particularly in the media, official statistics such as police data are viewed as accurate indicators of crime. Anyone who holds this view would be particularly inclined to consider Mary's experience atypical, because one rarely finds similar forms of violent female victimization in rural police and court data sets (DeKeseredy, Schwartz, et al. 2006; Scott et al. 2007). Unfortunately, under the best of circumstances official statistics are notoriously poor at reflecting all types of woman abuse, including the separation and divorce sexual assault that receives considerable attention in this book. Generally, official statistics do not count a crime as having happened unless someone (the victim, a neighbor) calls the police to report it, and the police agree to fill out a report stating that the event probably occurred. Rural communities have characteristics that make it even less likely that women will report abuse (Carrington 2007). Among these: the acceptance of stereotypical gender roles, that is, it is the role of women to stay with their husbands even if they are mistreated (Little 2003); geographic and social isolation, such as from social services or victim support (Averill, Padilla, and Clements 2007; Logan et al. 2006; Logan, Walker, and Leukefeld,

2001); the absence of public transportation (Lewis 2003); and a lack of economic opportunities that makes it much harder for the dependent spouse to rise up and gain a measure of independence.

This lack of support and opportunity may not affect the ability of rural communities to reduce most types of crime, such as burglary or robbery. In fact, Websdale (1998) argues that rural areas are characterized by social forces that have generally kept violent crime to levels below those experienced in urban areas. Here he is referring to social norms and attitudes that prevent such crimes as stranger rape and aggravated assault. His theory is based on the argument that the reason is rural patriarchal relations, including the existence of a powerful ol' boys network that among other things keeps some crime in check.

However, these same factors may increase the total amount of interpersonal violence within family or household settings (Osgood and Chambers 2000). Thus, Gagne (1992) reported in her study of Appalachian women that many of them not only were victimized, but also were convinced that they (at least temporarily) had no alternative but to put up with oppressive conditions, even as severe as those described by an abused woman interviewed by Maria Crawford and Rosemary Gartner who came very close to being killed by her male partner and is alive "by the grace of God" (1992, 142; see box 1.2).

Again, Gagne's respondents knew that the local police could be friends with abusers, which is also a major problem in rural parts of Australia and Canada (Carrington 2007; DeKeseredy 2007b).

Others, following in Websdale's (1998) path, argue that it is not specifics such as knowing local police officers that combine to make conditions oppressive for women, but that it is the very nature of rurality, which is based on male standards (Hogg and Carrington 2006), making women generally invisible when decisions are made (Alston 2003). This concept has been important in a variety of studies on rurality in recent years, which "have demonstrated how male dominance and supremacy are displayed through symbolic leisure activities as well as more severe manifestations of control (sometimes violent)" (Little and Panelli 2003, 283). Interpersonal violence for these men may be a form of proving to themselves and others their essential masculinity and heterosexuality, at least as they define it (Carrington, 2007; DeKeseredy, Donnermeyer, et al., 2007).[5]

1.2 Francine's Rural Experiences

In November, we moved into the country. There were no neighbors at all; it was isolated, desolate, and lonely. It snowed every day. My son was born in January of 1982. I had no washing machine, and I had to wash all the clothes and diapers by hand, in cold water. Maurice really liked this. I worked hard all day, I had no friends, I lost weight, and I became depressed. I hated being in the country, and being so isolated. A little while later, we realized the house was infested with rats; because of this, eventually we had to move back into town. We never had any visitors or friends. When we moved, he made me carry all the heaviest boxes and made me carry pieces of furniture by myself. I remained depressed, I kept to myself, and I felt very lonely.

Source: Crawford and Gartner 1992, 144.

Moreover, in rural areas there is a greater distrust of government, which means that even when crimes like wife beating or marital rape occur, the victim may be less likely than her urban counterpart to want the police involved (Hogg and Carrington 2006; Weisheit, Falcone, and Wells 2006). If rural areas are characterized by less crime generally, but that crime is more likely to be against acquaintances and violent, and rural patriarchy serves to encourage men's feelings of control and power over women, then we would expect to find a high degree of physical and sexual assault against intimate partners in rural areas. While it is far beyond the ability of this book to answer convincingly and scientifically the relative rate of sexual violence in rural areas against intimate partners, as opposed to urban communities, it is an area that we feel can be investigated, more for in-depth examination than for findings that can be easily generalized.

Purpose of This Book

This book contributes to the expansion of rural crime research and puts gender at the forefront of analysis, as do the studies reviewed by rural criminologists Donnermeyer, Jobes, and Barclay (2006). Above all, the research described here supports Susan Lewis's (2003, 31) assertion that "in many rural communities, there are hidden crimes, unspoken crimes, that are often hushed and sometimes ignored, crimes of sexual violence that require sensitivity and understanding to promote safety and justice." Although we focus on various types of woman abuse in rural communities, we pay special attention to sexual assault that takes place in the context of marital separation or divorce. The rationale for this focus is as follows. First, over the past thirty-five years there have been hundreds of North American studies of physical, sexual, and psychological woman abuse in marital and cohabiting relationships (Brownridge and Halli, 2001). All of them show that male-to-female victimization in these heterosexual unions is a major public health problem. And what is to be done about this brutal ongoing threat to women's health and safety? Criminal justice officials, shelter workers, and scores of others contend that these women's most important weapon in the battle to end their abuse is to divorce or separate from their partners (Schwartz 1988; Walker et al. 2004). Large numbers of women in abusive marital or cohabiting relationships continue to live in these "dangerous domains" for reasons beyond their control, such as economic dependency (H. Johnson 1996; Websdale and Johnson 2005). Most battered women eventually "flee the house of horrors," but separation or divorce alone often does not make them safer (Schwartz, 1989; Sev'er 2002).[6]

Many men will not leave their ex-partners alone, and their visits can be lethal. As Polk (2003, 134) reminds us: "Time and time again the phrase 'if I can't have you, no one will' echoes through the data on homicide in the context of sexual intimacy." For example, in 16 percent of the cases of intimate femicide that occurred in Ontario, Canada, between 1974 and 1994, the victims were separated from their legal spouses (Gartner, Dawson, and Crawford 2001).[7] Furthermore, throughout Canada, compared to women living with their partners, women who are separated run a sixfold risk of being killed (Wilson and Daly 1994). Separation is a key risk factor of femicide in the United States, as well (Bancroft 2002; Block 2000). In fact, in the United States close to 50 percent of men on death row for domestic murder killed their wives or lovers in retaliation for their leaving (Rapaport 1994; Stark 2007).

Every day in the United States, approximately four women are killed by a male intimate partner (Stout 2001). Moreover, statistics analyzed by the Chicago Women's Health Risk Study show that of fifty-nine women killed, 23 percent were leaving or trying to leave their partner during or just prior to their death. Seventeen percent of the women had already left and their partners were trying to "renew the relationship." This study also found that male sexual rivalry sometimes plays a role in intimate femicide. In one case examined, an ex-boyfriend said, as he murdered his female ex-partner and her new boyfriend, "If I can't have her, no one can" (Block 2000, 239). Indeed, data presented here and elsewhere support Diana E. H. Russell's (2001, 176) claim that femicide is "some men's 'final solution' for women."

Women who exit or try to leave relationships in the United States are also at high risk of being the targets of violence that does not result in death. For instance, Fleury, Sullivan, and Bybee (2000) found that more than one-third of the 135 women who participated in their longitudinal study were assaulted by a male ex-partner during a two-year period. Similarly, 40 percent of the 75 divorced men who participated in Arendell's (1995) study stated that they threatened or used violence against their former spouses after separation. Separated and divorced women are much more likely to experience nonfatal violence than are married women, according to recent data generated by the U.S. National Crime Victimization Survey. For example, the 2005 victimization rate per 1,000 females was 8.5 for divorced women, 49 for separated women, and 0.9 for married women (U.S. Bureau of Justice Statistics 2007).

Nonlethal separation assault is also common in Canada. Statistics Canada's national Violence against Women Survey found that about one-fifth (19 percent) of the women who reported violence by a previous male partner stated that the violence increased in severity at the time of separation (Johnson and Sacco 1995; Rodgers 1994), and 2004 Canadian General Social Survey data show that, among women with a former husband or male cohabiting partner who had been violent during the relationship, 49 percent were assaulted by their ex-partners after separation (Mihorean 2005). Several other North American studies, most of which are Canadian, uncovered similar data, with the risk of assault peaking in the first two months following separation and when women attempt permanent separation through legal or other means (DeKeseredy 2007b). It is no wonder that many of Evan Stark's female clients told him that "they were never more frightened than in the days, weeks, or months after they moved out" (2007, 116).

Of course, separation/divorce assaults are not restricted to North America. For example, McMurray et al. (2000) found that 21 percent of the 146 separated Western Australian men in their sample were violent during separation. Thus, as Douglas Brownridge (2006, 517) points out in his in-depth review of the international social scientific literature on violence against women postseparation:

> In short, studies that allow a comparison of violence among separated, divorced, and married women show a consistent pattern of separated and divorced women being at elevated risk for violence compared to married women, with separated women having by the far the greatest risk for post-separation violence. It appears that separated women have as much as thirty times the likelihood, and divorced women have as much as nine times the likelihood, of reporting non-lethal violence compared to married women.

Sexual assaults also occur when women are wanting to end, are planning to end, are trying to end, are in the process of ending, or have ended a relationship with a male marital or cohabiting partner (see box 1.3). For example, Fleury, Sullivan, and Bybee (2000) found that of the 49 women in their sample who were assaulted by an ex-partner, 20 percent were raped. Still, less than a handful of North American studies have focused on sexual assault during and after exits from relationships, and most of these data appear in the sparse feminist literature on what is variously termed marital rape, spousal rape, wife rape, or sexual assault in marriage (DeKeseredy, Rogness, and Schwartz 2004). Moreover, almost all the qualitative or quantitative empirical work on separation and divorce sexual assault was done in urban areas such as Boston, Chicago, and San Francisco (e.g., Block and DeKeseredy 2007; Finkelhor and Yllo 1985; Kurz 1995; Russell 1990). This book thus helps fill two major research gaps by presenting the results of an exploratory qualitative study of separation and divorce sexual assault in three rural Ohio communities.

Still, it is important to keep in mind that much, if not most, of the information offered in this book is "not news to battered women" (Stark 2007, 116). As Stark (2007, 116) correctly points out: "Abused women are much less likely than the professionals whose help they seek to regard decisions about physical proximity as means to end abuse and much more likely to regard separation as a tactical maneuver that carries a calculated risk

1.3 AN EPISODE OF SEPARATION / DIVORCE SEXUAL ASSAULT

One of Ann's attempts to leave resulted in her being taken for a ride to a remote nature conservation area, some hours' drive north of where she lived. Rob's stated goal was reconciliation. Ann had gone along with his offer because she took it to be genuine. The ride was not smooth, because Ann did not immediately give in to Rob's reconciliation request. This was quite unlike Ann. Previously she would have readily given into whatever Rob wanted. Ann was generally obedient, but on that hot and humid summer day, she did not immediately comply. Ann complained and asked Rob to treat her better. For her resistance, Rob's revenge was quite merciless. He stopped the van in the middle of the road, dragged Ann out into the bush, and violently raped her. The brush was sticky, and they were in the middle of the wilderness.

The rape was only the beginning of hours of torture that Rob inflicted on Ann. He ripped off all her clothes, jumped into his van, and started to drive away. Ann chased the van, totally exposed while he drove ahead, watching her anguish from the rearview mirror. Ann ran for seven miles. "It was a marshy area, the road was full of slithery things; he knew that I was deadly afraid of slithery things! I was hysterical." When Ann collapsed from her ordeal of the rape, coupled with her fear of the bush land and heat exhaustion, Rob picked up her nude body, drove back to the city, and dumped her on the front lawn of her parents' home.

Source: Sev'er 2002, 99–100.

within the orbit circumscribed by assault or coercive control. The disjunction between what victims and outsiders expect from separation remains a major obstacle to effective intervention and communication in the field."

DEFINITION OF RURAL

The first problem in any study of rural communities is to attempt to grasp the notion of what "rural" could mean (Scott et al. 2007). "Like concepts such as 'truth,' 'beauty,' or 'justice,' everyone knows the term rural, but no one can define it very precisely" (Weisheit, Falcone, and Wells

1994, 6). Even some of the most basic ideas are still somewhat at issue. For example, even though rural culture has not been studied much, traditional literature emphasizes a rural-urban difference in Western society. Some scholars argue that this dichotomy is no longer useful, or only partly useful, since the standardization of education, communication, and transportation has removed the unique aspects of rural culture (Donnermeyer, Jobes, and Barclay 2006). Those who still believe in a unique rural culture presume that a major difference is that there is more homogeneity in rural areas than in cities, leading to more collective control on deviant behavior (Hogg and Carrington 2003; Websdale 1998). Criminologists who accept official statistics as valid have argued that there is less overall crime in rural areas, and that the greatest rural/urban difference in this arena lies in the extent of violent crime. The difference is particularly striking in robbery rates (Weisheit, Falcone, and Wells 2006). That rural areas are homogenous, however, has been sharply challenged in recent years by those who argue that there are different types of rural communities, and important variations among these communities (Donnermeyer, Jobes, and Barclay 2006; Lee 2008). For instance, Jobes et al. (2004) found six different kinds of rural communities, ranging up to the highly disorganized small community with high crime rates.

Of course, not all rural communities are alike and, as Websdale (1998, 40) notes, "ultimately, the definition of rural communities is arbitrary and open to debate." Nevertheless, as DeKeseredy, Donnermeyer et al. (2007) remind us, four things are common in most, but not all, criminological conceptualizations of places identified as rural. Although these characteristics are true to a certain extent, they must be considered with care as they also can produce stereotypical images that suppress serious discussion of all types of crime and related issues in the rural context.

First, rural places have smaller populations and lower population densities. Second, people who live in rural areas are more likely to "know each other's business, come into regular contact with each other, and share a larger core of values than is true of people in urban areas" (Websdale 1995, 102). This characteristic can be referred to as a higher density of acquaintanceship, collective efficacy, or gemeinschaft, even though each term conveys a slightly different meaning in the sociological and criminological literatures (Amato 1993; Cancino 2005; Freudenburg 1986).[8] Third, in this postmodern era, rural communities are much less autonomous than before (Scott et al. 2007). And fourth, the standardization of education, along with other factors such as communication, has removed some of the unique features of rural culture and narrowed the difference between rural and urban lifestyles, as stated earlier (Fischer 1995; Krannich and Luloff 2002; Ritzer 2008; Rogers et al. 1988). Not long ago, a person in the United States could be rural poor and generally unaware of the comparative lack ("I Was a Coal-Miner's Daughter," not untypically of country and western music, for instance, tells of a family that was happy despite being poor). Today, TV alone makes it impossible for the poor to be unaware that many people have much better housing, furniture, clothes and even shoes than they have. Cultural, social, and economic divides are much more obvious in the rural United States than ever before. Other forces that affect rural areas include cultural, economic, and social factors; proximity to cities; presence of industries with absentee ownership; tourism; and the development policies of nation-states (Donnermeyer, Jobes, and Barclay 2006).

In sum, then (following DeKeseredy, Donnermeyer et al. 2007), rather than overloading a definition of "rural" to reflect social and cultural features that promote idyllic images and suppress the rural realities of crime, we use a nominal conceptualization of the term. Here, rural communities are places with small population sizes and/or densities that exhibit variable levels of collective efficacy. Likewise, we and other scholars with expertise on rural crime (e.g., Donnermeyer, Jobes, and Barclay 2006), make no generalized assumptions about the relationship of collective efficacy and crime in rural communities. Depending on both the rural community and the kind of crime under consideration, collective efficacy may increase or decrease crime. However, in this book, we present substantial evidence from our research and other studies of rural woman abuse that male peer support, neighbor nonintervention, and rural norms of patriarchy and privacy—all expressions of collective efficacy (not of social disorganization)—are significant contributors to the victimization of women.

CONCEPTUALIZATION OF SEPARATION AND DIVORCE

Is it essential for a couple to be living apart to be considered separated or divorced? Many surveys of marital rape and nonsexual types of woman abuse seem to define separation and divorce this way. While this approach may reflect common sense, it neglects assaults that are committed after a woman makes a decision to leave a relationship, or makes an unsuccessful attempt to leave a relationship that she is locked into (Mahoney 1991; Ptacek 1999). Many men have a "fanatical determination" to prevent their spouses or live-in partners from leaving and will use violence "to keep them in their place" (Russell 1990). These are some of the key reasons why Mahoney (1991, 65–66) prefers the term "separation assault," which she defines as "the attack on the woman's body and volition in which her partner seeks to prevent her from leaving, retaliate for the separation, or force her to return. It aims at overbearing her will as to where and with whom she will live, and coercing her in order to enforce connection in a relationship. It is an attempt to gain, retain, or regain power in a relationship, or to punish the woman for ending the relationship. It often takes place over time."

Although rarely considered in this vein, a woman's decision to leave a relationship may be long and complex, as domestic violence scholars have long known (Goetting 1999). She may feel simultaneously oppressed and trapped by an inability to leave a relationship right now. This may be for financial or economic reasons, or because she has been unable to make adequate arrangements to care for her children, or for a variety of other reasons. For example, a forty-nine-year-old woman from a small Ohio farming town told us about a member of her community who was permanently trapped in an abusive relationship:

> I went down and done some wallpapering for her. And she's in her eighties and she was talking to me and of course her and her husband know my husband real well and she says, "Susan, let me tell you." She says, "If you can get out, get out. You're still young enough." She says, "I'm setting here waiting to die." She says, "I'm too old to get out," and she says she takes abuse every day. And I said, "You don't have to do that." And she says, "What am I gonna do?" And these are, these are farming people, this community is a farming community. And the way the things are set up with farming and stuff like that, you have no money, access to money. You have nothing. And you know if a woman wants out, she has to have plenty of money hid someplace 'cause she's not gonna get no help in this county. I don't know how it is in other counties, but this county you don't. It's a, it's a disgrace.

Many women defy men's patriarchal control by emotionally separating from them. Emotional separation, a major predictor of a permanent end to a relationship, is a women's denial or restriction of sexual relations and other intimate exchanges (Ellis and DeKeseredy 1997). Emotionally exiting a relationship can be just as dangerous as physically or legally exiting one because it, too, increases the likelihood of male violence and sexual abuse (Block and DeKeseredy 2007). For example, of the one hundred sexually abused women who participated in McFarlane and Malecha's (2005) study sponsored by the National Institute of Justice, 22 percent reported an emotional separation before the first time they were sexually assaulted.

Separation and divorce are not functions only of proximity, and a woman does not have to be legally tied to a man to experience sexual or physical assault (Bergen 1996; Block and DeKeseredy 2007). Brownridge and Halli's (2001) review of fourteen studies (eight done in the United States, five in Canada, and one in New Zealand) reveals "quite dramatic" differences in violence rates obtained from married persons and cohabitors. In fact, they found the rate of violence for cohabitors typically twice that of married persons, but as great as four times higher. Compared to married women, It is not only the rate of violence where cohabiting women are at a disadvantage; the severity of this violence is also much worse for them than for their married counterparts. In another example, Canadian national survey data show that many women are sexually abused by their common-law partners, and male cohabitors are more likely to sexually abuse their partners than are men in casual or serious dating relationships (DeKeseredy and Schwartz 1998b).

These are not the only studies that identify male cohabitors as more likely to be sexually abusive than married men. For example, Finkelhor and Yllo (1985) found that 23 percent of the women in their sample who separated from cohabitors experienced forced sex, compared to 3 percent of married women. Fully 25 percent of the women who reported forced sex were legally separated or divorced.

Based on the foregoing findings and data presented elsewhere (e.g., DeKeseredy, Rogness, and Schwartz 2004), "separation and divorce" here means physically, legally, or emotionally exiting a marital or cohabiting relationship. This project focused on women-initiated separations and divorces because "they are the decisions that challenge male hegemony the most" (Sev'er 1997, 567).

Definition of Sexual Assault

We use here a broad definition of sexual assault because it, like the physical and psychological abuse of women, takes many shapes and forms. (The major problems with narrow definitions of sexual assault have been covered elsewhere [DeKeseredy 2000].) Unlike that of many studies of sexual assault, our definition is not restricted to acts of forced penetration. Many women experience a wide range of sexually abusive behaviors, such as assaults when they are drunk or high, or when they are legally unable to give consent (Bachar and Koss 2001; Schwartz and Leggett 1999). Married and cohabiting women also experience threats that can result in painful unwanted sex and "blackmail rapes." Consider the following description by "Mrs. Brown" (Russell 1990, 338). Just because there was no threat or actual use of force does not mean that her experience was not terrifying, emotionally scarring, or highly injurious, and she labels as rape this assault by her first husband:

> The worst raping occasion was in the morning I awoke in labor with my first child. The hospital I was booked into was a thirty-minute drive away, and this being the first time I had undergone childbirth, I had no idea of how close I was to giving birth, or what was to happen to me next. I labored at home for a few hours until perhaps 11:00 A.M., and then said to my ex-husband that I thought we'd better go to the hospital. The pains were acute and I was panicking that I would not be able to bear them. He looked at me, and said, "Oh, all right. But we'd better have a screw first, because it'll be a week before you're home again." I couldn't believe it, even of him. "Please, W., take me to the hospital," I begged as another contraction stormed across my body. "Not until we have a screw," he insisted. I wept, I cried, I pleaded, but he wouldn't budge. The pleading went on until midday, by which time I was frantic to get nursing help. He stood adamant with his arms crossed, a smirk on his face, and jiggling the car keys as a bribe. In the end I submitted. It took two minutes, then we dressed and drove to the hospital. The baby was born five hours later.

Most definitions of sexual assault also exclude unwanted sex that occurs "out of a sense of obligation" (Bergen 1996), sexual relations that stem from ex-partners' threats of fighting for sole custody of children,

and other sexual acts that do not involve the use of threats of force.[9] One
of our respondents talks about unwanted sex that occurs out of women's
sense of obligation:

> Um, I think that our society, um, that, um, this community that we
> live in and the society that we live in is, um, male dominated in
> general. And so, um, everything from our media to our family and
> peer experiences influences the way we, the way women view
> ourselves. I see many, many, many women submitting to men, . . .
> submitting to what they, their men want them to be. I have had many,
> many discussions, over a hundred, women saying to me, my boyfriend
> wants to have sex, but I don't want to have sex, but I am going to
> do it anyway to please him. And so, I consider that unwanted sex,
> because, yes, these women are consenting, but they don't know any
> other out. They have no other option. And that is what I find sad.
> And there is so much peer influence about being cool, about being
> heterosexual, you know?

Agnes provides a similar account of such unwanted sex:

> So there might be some entitlement that the husband feels. The
> woman feeling that it's easier to give in, especially for the kids. A lot
> of social norms, I guess, social pressure to where the woman takes on
> a passive role sexually. It's not a big deal. It'll be over soon. That's not
> addressing a solution other than a marriage counselor or someone
> that she goes to for help could address that issue of where you're
> going to be and how you're going handle and come up with a plan.

Excluding from a definition of sexual assault the abusive behaviors
identified here exacerbates the problem of underreporting and ultimately
underestimates the extent of sexual assault. Thus, guided by Koss, Gidycz,
and Wisniewski's (1987, 166) conceptual and empirical work, here is how
we classified the types of sexual assault described by forty-three rural Ohio
interviewees:

Sexual contact includes sex play (fondling, kissing, or petting)
    arising from menacing verbal pressure, misuse of authority,
    threats of harm, or actual physical force.

Sexual coercion includes unwanted sexual intercourse arising from the use of menacing verbal pressure or the misuse of authority.

Attempted rape includes attempted unwanted sexual intercourse arising from the use of or threats of force, or the use of drugs or alcohol.

Rape includes unwanted sexual intercourse arising from the use of or threats of force and other unwanted sex acts (anal or oral intercourse or penetration by objects other than the penis) arising from the use of or threat of force, or the use of drugs or alcohol.

CONCEPTUALIZATION OF MALE PEER SUPPORT

Our study identifies one of the key risk factors for sexual assault of rural women as patriarchal male peer support, which is defined as "attachments to male peers and the resources they provide which encourage and legitimate woman abuse" (DeKeseredy 1990, 130). Except for Websdale's (1998) Kentucky study, no empirical attempt has been made to discern the existence, nature, and content of pro-abuse male social networks in rural U.S. communities.[10] In fact, most male peer support research is quantitative in nature and limited to explaining violence on college campuses. Moreover, prior to our research, no study concentrated on whether male peer support contributes to sexual assault during or after the termination of any type of intimate relationship. Thus, another key objective of this book is to enhance a sociological understanding of the ways in which sexist male peer group dynamics perpetuate and justify the sexual abuse of separated/divorced rural women.

THE NEED FOR POLICY-RELEVANT DATA

Our study is much more than an empirical enterprise. Of course, one of the major goals is to enhance a social scientific understanding of a problem that has garnered limited attention from the media, the scientific community, and the criminal justice system. However, we are equally concerned with generating policy-relevant data that can be used to design more effective prevention and social support services for a group of women who continue to suffer in silence. Again, too often, separation/divorce does not end abuse; thus it is necessary to develop policies and practices that meet the unique needs of women who are terrorized by sexual violence during and after the process of leaving marital and cohabiting relationships. "There is often a failure on behalf of others including police officers, religious advisors, battered women's shelter advocates, and rape crisis counselors to provide adequate assistance," as Bergen (2006, 6) discovered.

Like Ptacek's study of battered women in the courtroom, as well as the growing body of U.S. research on the abuse of poor and minority women, this book simultaneously helps shift the "experiences of the most economically and politically marginalized women to the center of the analysis" and responds to scholarly requests to move beyond the "urban-exclusive orientation of criminology" (Ptacek 1999, 39; Donnermeyer, Jobes, and Barclay 2006, 199).[11] Of special concern is the plight of rural women who are sexually assaulted when they want to leave, are trying to leave, are in the process of leaving, or have left their intimate male partners.

The rural Ohio women who shared their stories with us are heroes, struggling to survive what looks like a never-ending "war on women" (Vallee 2007). This statement is not an exaggeration, given that every woman we interviewed was at great risk of being killed by her ex-partner. Unfortunately, what Stark (1993, 667) stated fifteen years ago in his commentary on urban research still holds true and is directly relevant to an understanding of the rural data presented in subsequent chapters: "separated and divorced women face the greatest risk of severe ongoing violence, including homicide."

OUTLINE OF THIS BOOK

The next chapter presents the theoretical framework that guided our study. In chapter 3, we briefly describe the research settings and the methods we used to gather the data scattered throughout this book. Here we pay special attention to the broad political, economic, and social contexts in which we carried out our study. In chapter 4, we present our findings on the types and timing of separation/divorce assault, as well as on how factors such as patriarchal control, male peer support, and male consumption of pornography contribute to victimization. In chapter 5, we provide data on the consequences of separation/divorce abuse and rural Ohio women's social support experiences. Finally, we discusses the empirical, theoretical, and policy implications of our study in chapter 6.

CHAPTER 2

Thinking Theoretically about Separation and Divorce Sexual Assault

It's a big problem. And a lot of people get by with it.
—Joan, rural Ohio interviewee

NORTH AMERICAN DATA on the prevalence of separation and divorce sexual assault may not be plentiful, but the limited amount available shows that just before, during, and after terminating a relationship with a spouse or cohabitor are dangerous times.[1] As an abused woman interviewed by journalist Tracy Huffman explained, "Leaving was only a small part. What I had to face afterward was much bigger" (2005). Many other women had, and continue to have, similar experiences. For example:

> Eight percent of the wife rape survivors in Russell's (1990) San Francisco survey were assaulted after their marriages ended, and 7 percent were raped just before separation.

> Seventeen percent of the divorced women interviewed by Kurz (1995) reported that their ex-husbands forced them to have sex.

> Twenty percent of the forty wife rape survivors interviewed by Bergen (1996) were raped after separation or divorce.

> Two-thirds of the women in Finkelhor and Yllo's (1985) interview sample (N = 50) were raped in the last days of a relationship, either after previous separations, or when they were trying to leave a relationship.

A more recent and much larger study—the U.S. National Violence Against Women Survey (VAWS)—tested the hypothesis that sexual assault is more likely to occur following separation or divorce from either spouses or cohabitors. Based on their analysis of their findings, the principal investigators contend that "most rapes . . . perpetrated against women by intimates occur in the context of ongoing rather than terminated relationships" (Tjaden and Thonnes 2000, 37–38). At first glance, VAWS data support this claim because only 6.3 percent of the total number of rape victims (N = 288) stated that they were raped after the relationship ended.

Similarly, using data generated by the Chicago Women's Health Risk Study, Block and DeKeseredy (2007) found that abused women in violent relationships reported more forced sex than did women who leave such relationships (25.5 percent vs. 12.5 percent). These figures were the only ones we could find in the relevant literature that show that women in ongoing relationships are more likely to be sexually assaulted than those who are separated or divorced. This is not surprising for several reasons directly relevant to the issue of defining separation and divorce sexual assault. For example, VAWS researchers and Block and DeKeseredy (2007) used narrow definitions of sexual assault and thus excluded a broad range of harmful sexual behaviors experienced by many women. In fact, all the estimates just listed would be higher if the definition of sexual assault used was broader and common-law relationships were more carefully examined. Note, too, most of these studies were specifically designed to examine marital rape, and respondents were not asked a variety of specific questions about rape after separation and divorce. If these questions had been asked, the rates of separation and divorce sexual assault would be higher.

Our study, albeit not a survey, was explicitly designed to help fill some gaps in the empirical literature on separation and divorce sexual assault. However, we are equally concerned with advancing a better theoretical understanding of the problem. In this chapter, we describe the perspective that guided our research. A basic problem is that since the 1990s a growing number of international scholars have expanded rural crime research, but the bulk of their theoretical and empirical work is still not informed by any variant of critical criminological thought (e.g., feminism, left realism, cultural criminology, etc.).[2] Although various definitions of critical criminology have been proposed, there is no widely accepted precise formulation. For the purpose of this book, however, we define critical criminology as a broad perspective that views the major sources of crime as the class, ethnic, and patriarchal relations that control our society.[3] Further, critical criminology rejects as solutions to crime short-term measures such as tougher laws, increased incarceration, coercive counseling therapy, and the like. Rather, critical criminologists regard major structural and cultural changes within society as essential steps to reduce criminality and to promote social justice (DeKeseredy and Perry 2006b).

Like many other types of criminological inquiry, rural research on crime and its control is also, for the most part, "gender blind" (Gelsthorpe and Morris 1988). Consider rural studies cited in Donnermeyer, Jobes, and Barclay's (2006) extensive literature review. Only a few focus specifically on gender issues (e.g., woman abuse and societal reactions to this harm), and less than a handful of the scholars who conducted these studies publicly identify themselves as critical criminologists.[4] In this book, following Kathleen Daly and Meda Chesney-Lind (1988, 502) and other feminist scholars, we do not equate gender with sex. Rather, like Edwin Schur (1984, 10), we refer to gender as "the sociocultural and psychological shaping, patterning, and evaluating of male and female behavior."

Certainly, rural crime research has yet to develop a critical theoretical framework that can synthesize current scholarship on what Hogg and Carrington (2006, 171) refer to as "gendered violence and the architecture of rural life." Further, the limited theoretical work that does exist on this topic ignores separation and divorce sexual assault. Of course, the neglect on the part of scholars to examine this problem applies to woman abuse research in general. Here, then, to help fill the gap in the rural crime literature, we propose an empirically informed theory that allows for a simultaneous consideration of broader macrolevel forces and microlevel gender relations of central concern to feminist scholars. Our offering moves well beyond answering the problematic question, "Why doesn't she leave?" to "What happens when she leaves or tries to leave?" and "Why do men do it?" (Hardesty 2002, 599; Stark 2007).[5]

A FEMINIST/MALE PEER SUPPORT MODEL
OF SEPARATION AND DIVORCE SEXUAL ASSAULT

Why do men sexually assault female partners who want to leave
them or who have left them? Given the absence of data on the motivations of men who engage in separation and divorce sexual assault, it is
not surprising that there are no theories specifically designed to answer
this question. Even the marital rape literature is essentially atheoretical,
because it is restricted to presenting women's opinions about why their
partners assaulted them or to constructing typologies based on the information provided by female respondents (DeKeseredy et al. 2004;
Mahoney and Williams 1998). For example, Finkelhor and Yllo (1985)
identified three types of marital rape: battering rape, force-only rape, and
obsessive rape. This and other typologies of marital rape (e.g., Bergen
1996, 2006; Russell 1990) have been reviewed elsewhere (see Mahoney
and Williams 1998).

The foregoing observations should not be construed as an all-out
indictment of this limited theoretical work. Certainly, marital rape
researchers have identified several important risk factors (e.g., power,
control, adherence to the ideology of familial patriarchy), which is a
significant step toward constructing and testing theories of separation
and divorce sexual assault, as well as other variants of woman abuse
(Jasinski 2001). In fact, we included in the theoretical model that
informed our rural Ohio study some of the determinants mentioned by
participants in marital rape studies done by Bergen (1996), Russell
(1990), and others (e.g., Finkelhor and Yllo 1985). Described in figure
2.1 and developed by DeKeseredy, Rogness, and Schwartz (2004), this
model is also guided by the theoretical literature on nonsexual forms of
violence (e.g., beatings, homicide, etc.) that occur when women want
to exit or have left a relationship.

Central to all this work is the role of patriarchal dominance and
control, which is also a major theme in the marital rape literature
(Bergen 2006). For example, McKenzie Rogness's (2003) integrated
theory contends that macrolevel factors like societal patriarchy work
together with microlevel forces such as patriarchal male peer support to
influence men to rape their marital/cohabiting partners. Guided by her
perspective and Jana Jasinski's (2001) call for "acknowledging the existence of multiple risk factors" when doing theoretical work on woman

abuse in general, societal patriarchy, "male proprietariness" (Wilson and Daly 1992), and patriarchal male peer support are major components of our theoretical model (figure 2.1).[6] Here, we discuss these and other variables included in it.

Societal Patriarchy

Despite the fact that psychological perspectives on woman abuse are not as popular among criminologists as they were in the 1970s, several researchers still claim that the majority of men who beat, kill, or sexually assault their current or estranged female intimate partners do so because they are mentally ill or suffer from personality disorders (e.g., Dutton 2006).[7] Much of the popular British sensibility on battered women was formed on the parallel theory, popularized by J. J. Gayford

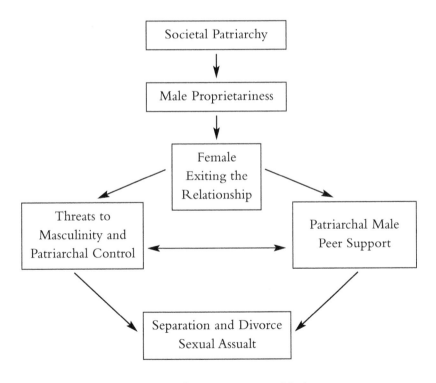

2.1 A Feminist / Male Peer Support Model of Separation
and Divorce Sexual Assault

(1975), that the women themselves can be seen as deviant or mentally ill, thus bringing the violence upon themselves.[8]

It is difficult for many people to view men such as those who assaulted the women who participated in our study as anything other than sick. However, this perspective lacks empirical support for several reasons. Certainly, woman abuse is occasionally a function of psycho-pathology; still, a large body of research shows that most abusive men are "less pathological than expected" (Gondolf 1999). Further, large- and small-scale North American studies show that woman abuse occurs regularly in a wide variety of intimate relationships. For example, Canadian and U.S. surveys that used some form of the Conflict Tactics Scale (CTS) show that at least 11 percent of the women in marital/cohabiting relationships are physically abused by their male partners on an annual basis (DeKeseredy 2009).[9]

As described by Faludi (1991), Hammer (2002), and many others who made progressive contributions to an interdisciplinary under-standing of the enduring discrimination against contemporary U.S. women, we still live in a political economic climate characterized by vitriolic attacks on feminist scholarship, practice, and activism that are intended to secure women's basic human rights (DeKeseredy and Dragiewicz 2007). Thus, it is not surprising that some antifeminist scholars, conservative fathers' rights groups, and others intent on margin-alizing the consideration of gender in the etiology of violence trivialize the extent of male-to-female violence described here and in many other publications. One tactic they use is claiming that women are as violent as men, which warrants brief attention here.

To support this claim, proponents of the sexual symmetry of violence thesis rely on CTS data that ignore the contexts, meanings, and motives of both men's and women's violence. As has been repeatedly stated, unless researchers can accurately determine why women use physical violence against men, it is irresponsible to contend, as Dutton (2006, ix) does, that, "in Canada and the United States, women use violence in intimate relationships to the same extent as men, for the same reasons, and with largely the same results."

To reach these conclusions, Dutton and other proponents of the sexual symmetry of violence thesis (e.g., Archer 2006) artificially narrow the definition of violence between intimates to obscure injurious behaviors that display marked sexual asymmetry, such as sexual assault, strangulation, separation assault, stalking, and homicide. Rather than an unacceptable or hysterical broadening of the definition of violence, these behaviors are commonly part of abused women's experience (DeKeseredy and Dragiewicz 2007). Those who contend that women are as violent as men downplay research on these forms of violence. Moreover, they seldom differentiate between defensive and offensive forms of violence between intimates, a courtesy extended to victims of other crimes (DeKeseredy 2006).

To make claims about the symmetry of violence between intimate partners, one must also conflate sex and gender. Discussions of prevalence that rely on the variables "male" and "female" cannot tell us much about gender, the socially constructed and normative set of meanings attached to these categories. This distinction is one of the primary contributions to the social sciences of feminist perspectives. Research that asks perpetrators and survivors about the nature of violence between intimates finds that both say much about gender. For example, violent men talk about threats to their masculinity they experience when women or men fail to demonstrate what they deem to be adequate respect for them, whereas women talk about the normative gender expectations that abusers use to justify their violence (DeKeseredy and Dragiewicz 2007).

If only a handful of North American men abused their current or former partners, it would be very easy to accept nonsociological and gender-blind accounts of their behaviors. They must be disturbed individuals. Unfortunately, in rural Ohio, as in other parts of the United States and in other advanced industrial nations (e.g., Canada), a substantial number of injurious male actions, values, and beliefs are microsocial expressions of broader patriarchal forces. Simply put, the problem is not one in which individual men all happen to suffer from the same psychopathology, or weak ego, or whatever. Rather, they all live in the same society, and the individual man is partly a reflection of the values and beliefs that are expressed by the broader society. As Jackson Katz (2006, 28) notes in his analysis of men who abuse women: "Most men who assault women are not so much disturbed as they are disturbingly *normal*. Like all of us, they are products of familial and social systems. They are our sons, brothers, friends, and coworkers. As such they are influenced not only by individual factors, but also by broader cultural attitudes and beliefs about manhood that shape their psyches and iden- tities. And *ours*" (emphasis in original).

As Katz also reminds us, most woman abusers are "our guys," which is the title of journalist Bernard Lefkowitz's book about a horrific crime that occurred in 1989 in Glen Ridge, New Jersey. At first glance, Glen Ridge appears to be "an affluent, idyllic suburb, the kind of town that exemplifies the American Dream" (Random House 2003, 2). If you went there for a visit, your first impression would probably be similar to Lefkowitz's (1997, 5–6): "My first mental snapshot: Glen Ridge was a squeaky-clean, manicured town that liked to display its affluence by dressing its high school graduates in dinner jackets and gowns. What impressed me the most was the orderliness of the place. The streets, the lawns, the houses—everything seemed in proportion. There were no excesses of bad taste, no evidence of neglect or disrepair."

In March 1989, something went terribly wrong in "paradise" (Random House 2003). Thirteen male athletes who attended Glen Ridge High School (actor Tom Cruise's alma mater) lured a mentally disabled girl into a basement, where four of them raped her with a base- ball bat and a broomstick while the others looked on. To make matters worse, it was weeks before anyone reported this crime to the police and years before the boys went to trial. Four of them were eventually convicted of various crimes. However, one of these was convicted only of a third-degree conspiracy charge and received a sentence of three years' probation and two hundred hours of community service. The other three were granted bail and remained free until their appeals were decided more than five years later.

Given the severity of the Glen Ridge gang rape, some people may contend that this case is an isolated incident. It is not. For example, a large literature shows that fraternity gang rapes and other similar crimes are frequently committed by "homegrown products of contemporary American society" (Katz 2006, 28).[10] An even larger scientific literature shows that sexual, physical, and psychological abuse is common in North American heterosexual relationships.[11] Again, men who abuse women are not acting in a deviant manner that completely violates everything they have ever learned about the way to treat women. Of course, some abusive men have clinical pathologies (O'Leary 1993), but most do not

(DeKeseredy and Schwartz 1996; Pagelow 1992, 1993). Some researchers even claim that mental disorders cause less than 10 percent of all incidents of intimate violence and that psychological perspectives cannot explain the other 90 percent (Gelles and Straus 1988).

Although a majority of men perhaps never sexually or physically assault women, certainly all North American men, including those who live in rural communities, live in a society that can accurately be termed a "rape culture" (Buchwald, Fletcher, and Roth 1993), where no man can avoid exposure to patriarchal and prorape attitudes. For example, rare is a man who has not been exposed to pornographic media, to mainstream television shows or movies depicting women as inferior to men, and to rap videos and songs referring to women as "bitches" and "hoes" (Katz 2006; Schwartz and DeKeseredy 1997). Further, as described by Antonia Zerbisias (see box 2.1), pornography produced and consumed in the United States is becoming more violent and increasingly "normalized" (R. Jensen 2007).

Our interview data show that pornography plays a major role in separation and divorce sexual assault. So does men's adherence to the ideology of familial patriarchy, a discourse that supports the abuse of women who violate the ideals of male power, as well as men's control over women in intimate relationships (DeKeseredy and Schwartz 1993; Smith 1990). Also relevant is familial patriarchy's insistence on women's obedience, respect, loyalty, dependency, sexual access, and sexual fidelity (Barrett and McIntosh 1982; DeKeseredy and Schwartz 1998b; Dobash and Dobash 1979; Pateman 1988).

Familial patriarchy is a subsystem of societal patriarchy. These two types of patriarchy cannot be pulled too far apart, and one cannot be fully understood without reference to the other (Smith 1990). Although the definition of societal patriarchy is the subject of much debate, here societal patriarchy refers to male domination at the societal level. Following Dobash and Dobash (1979), societal patriarchy is made up of two elements: a structure and an ideology. Structurally, the patriarchy is a hierarchical social organization in which males have more power and privilege than women have. Certainly, North America is well known for being a continent characterized by gross gender inequity. For example, laws in thirty U.S. states allow a man to receive conditional exemptions if he rapes his wife (Bergen 2006).[12] Moreover, despite decades of ongoing struggle and activism around the issue of pay equity, women earn about 73.25 percent of what men earn in the United States (Lips 2005). Note, too, that on October 3, 2006, Bev Oda, federal minister for the Status of Women Canada (SWC), announced that women's organizations would no longer be eligible for funding for advocacy, government lobbying, or research projects. Further, SWC was required to delete the word "equality" from its list of goals (Carastathis 2006). So much for Donald Dutton's (2006, ix) claim that "women rights have finally been acknowledged after centuries of religion-based political oppression."

2.1 PACKAGING ABUSE OF WOMEN AS ENTERTAINMENT FOR ADULTS: CRUEL, DEGRADING SCENES "NORMALIZE" FOR A GENERATION BROUGHT UP IN DOT-COM WORLD BY ANTONIA ZERBISIAS

The hottest place on Earth this month was Las Vegas.

That was the site of the AVN Adult Entertainment Expo where thousands of . . . exhibitors and fans of pornography came together to look at the latest in media, toys, games, gadgets, paraphernalia, and genitalia.

Yes, the pornography industrial complex is so huge that it can fill one of the world's biggest convention halls, so mainstream that it need no longer operate in the dirty raincoat section of your local newsstand or video store, so available that it's on basic cable, so accessible that any child could Google her way to Internet sites where women (and men and children) are brutalized for somebody's fun and profit.

According to the Internet Filter Review, worldwide porn revenues, including in-room movies at hotels, sex clubs and the ever-expanding E-sex world, topped $97 billion in 2006. That's more than the revenues of the top technology companies combined: Microsoft, Google, Amazon, eBay, Yahoo!, Apple, Netflix, and Earthlink. . . .

When I can easily find websites that show women subjected to what can only be described in a family newspaper as waterboarding by ejaculate—or simultaneous impalement on more than

Although the United States is a patriarchal country, some laws and other means of eliminating sexism have affected every major U.S. social institution—the family, the workplace, the military, and so on (Renzetti and Curran 2002). Nevertheless, as Stanko (1997, 630) observes: "Despite the advantages for some women who have achieved educational and employment recognition, our concern about physical and sexual integrity remains one of our main worries," because "there is little evidence that the general patterns of men's abuse have been interrupted."

one fire pole, or sexual practices that will cause *E. coli* infections—I have to wonder where the industry gets these ideas.

It's as if, just like TV reality shows, the fear factor/cruelty/shock value has to be continuously ratcheted up to get them into the tent, especially online. And make no mistake, when you see women being brutalized this way, you are not seeing an act. That woman really is gagging, really is gasping for air, really is drowning.

Every second, 28,258 Internet users are viewing pornography. Every second. That's a lot of women who . . . are being tortured.

Robert Jensen, a journalism professor at the University of Texas at Austin, has been tracking this trend for years. In his new book *Getting Off: Pornography and the End of Masculinity*, he writes with alarm how the "cruelty line" in mass-market pornography is driving up. At the same time, the "normalization" line—the measure of the acceptance of pornography in the mainstream contemporary culture—is also up, sharply.

"If pornography is increasingly cruel and degrading, why is it increasingly commonplace instead of more marginalized?" he writes. "In a society that purports to be civilized, wouldn't we expect most people to reject sexual material that becomes ever-more dismissive of the humanity of women? How do we explain the simultaneous appearance of more, and increasingly more intense, ways to humiliate women sexually and the rising popularity of the films that present those activities?"

Source: *Toronto Star*, January 26, 2008.

We could easily provide innumerable examples of patriarchal discourses and practices. Still, they do not answer a number of questions. Why do men maintain this power? Why don't they, in the spirit of fair play, simply give up enough power to equalize the power between men and women? Why don't more women rebel against the patriarchy? The answers lie in the other aspect of patriarchy: the ideology. The ideology of patriarchy provides a political and social rationale for its enduring. Both men and women who accept that ideology come to believe that it is "natural" and "right" that women be in inferior positions. Such men feel completely supported in excluding women, and up to a point such women feel that exclusion is correct (DeKeseredy and Schwartz 1993; Katz 2006). To a man or woman who believes completely in the ideology of patriarchy, the entire concept of equal rights or women's liberation is controversial and sounds not only wrong but unnatural (Bacchetta and Power 2002).

Male Proprietariness

We live in a patriarchal society that promotes male proprietariness, which we may define as "the tendency [of men] to think of women as sexual and reproductive 'property' they can own and exchange" (Wilson and Daly 1992, 85). For example, one survivor of wife rape interviewed by Raquel Bergen was frequently told by her abusive partner, "That's my body—my ass, my tits, my body. You gave that to me when you married me and that belongs to me" (Bergen 1996, 20). Similarly, one of our respondents was repeatedly sexually assaulted because, she explained, "it was his way of letting me know that, ah, first of all, of letting me know that I was his." And Jackie was often reminded, "You're my wife. You're my property."

Proprietariness refers to "not just the emotional force of [the male's] own feelings of entitlement but to a more pervasive attitude [of ownership and control] toward social relationships [with intimate female partners]" (Wilson and Daly 1992, 95). Indeed, many male threats to kill women are tactics the men use to terrorize their wives or cohabitors and to "keep them in line" (Barnard et al. 1982; Polk and Ranson 1991), signified by the horrifying words, "If I can't have her, no one can" (Serran and Firestone 2004, 3).

Often men combine such threats with violence, which is a form of informal social control (Black 1983; Ellis and DeKeseredy 1997). The use of violence as a means of social control escalates when female partners leave or attempt to leave a relationship, because exiting is an extreme public challenge to male partners who believe they own their wives or cohabiting partners and they have the right to control them (Block 2003). Even if relatively few women are actually killed by their ex-partners, most of them who receive death threats or who are victimized by nonlethal violence "live with the legacies of terror for the remainder of their lives" (Stanko 1997, 632). As one interviewee put it, "I wasn't safe anywhere."

Sometimes the victims of male proprietariness are not only the women seeking freedom, but also the women's prized possessions or people they deeply care for. Consider the following experiences reported by some of Aysan Sev'er's (1997, 580–581) interviewees:

> Laurette and Sue talked about the shattering of their treasured heirlooms in front of their eyes. Laurette's husband burned her books when she decided to take a few university courses. Daisy's husband slashed her favorite dress into ribbons so that she would not look pretty and "run away" with men. Ann's partner's violence extended to the cat she loved (and still keeps). He would raise the cat closer and closer to the revolving blades of the ceiling fan, and demand things that Ann did not want to do (such as swallowing large doses of sleeping pills). The partner kept her drowsy and docile and always told her that "she needed him."

Women's ex-partners often target their children as a means of regaining control (see box 2.2). In fact, for many abused women, the following factors contribute to a well-founded fear of exiting dangerous relationships:

> Abusers often threaten to charge their partner with kidnapping if they try to leave with the children. Women can be so isolated that they begin to believe much of what the abuser tells them.
>
> Abusers often threaten to sue for custody and threaten that the children's mother won't see them again.
>
> Women may fear that their children will be abducted or abused. (Conlin, Chapman, and Benson 2006, 37)

2.2 THE HIDDEN VICTIMS OF SEPARATION AND DIVORCE ABUSE

The hidden victims of abused women's difficulties in family court proceedings are the children. Children who have already been traumatized may be used [by abusers] in attempts to control the abused woman or as an excuse to have increased contact with her when she is attempting to create separation from the abuse. During family court proceedings and in the aftermath of poor outcomes, children can be placed in the center of the abusive relationship. When joint custody or poor access arrangements are established, the abused mother is forced into ongoing contact with the abuser creating safety issues, forcing her and the children to deal with controlling tactics and emotional abuse by the perpetrator. In extreme situations, women or children have been murdered by the abusive man. Luke's Place is named in memory of Luke, a three-year-old boy in Durham Region [in Ontario, Canada] who, on his first unsupervised access visit in August of 1997, was strangled and burned to death by his father. This unsupervised access was allowed by the family court process despite pleas from the child's mother to permit supervised access only.

Source: Luke's Place 2007, 4. Luke's Place serves the Durham Region in Ontario, Canada. It is the first Canadian resource and information center with the unique focus on supporting woman abuse survivors and their children as they deal with custody and access issues within the Ontario Family Court System. See *www.lukesplace.ca/contact_us.htm.*

Exiting the Relationship

Most women in abusive relationships or in nonviolent relationships characterized by other means of patriarchal dominance and control are not weak people who are unable to take steps on their own behalf. In fact, many women resist their male partners' proprietariness in a variety of ways, including doing what one woman told us: "With me being a strong-headed woman, I did not like that and I refused to cook for him, I refused to do his laundry. I told him to do it his damn self because I don't want to be his slave. He didn't like that. . . . That would usually have me end up with a fist in my face or my head bashed against a wall."

There are also many women who defy men's control by exiting or trying to exit a relationship, and this may involve separating emotionally, obtaining a separate residence, starting or completing a legal separation and divorce, or all of these. Regardless of how a woman does it, her attempt to exit or her successful departure from a sexist relationship challenges male proprietariness and may result in violence, including homicide (Dobash et al. 2007). As Lundy Bancroft (2002, 219), among others, demonstrate: "The abuser's dehumanizing view of his partner as a personal possession can grow even uglier as a relationship draws to a close." Still, exiting alone, like all single factors, cannot of itself account for sexual assault. For example, many abusive patriarchal men have male friends with similar beliefs and values, and these peers reinforce the notion that women's exiting is a threat to a man's masculinity (see chapter 4).

Patriarchal Male Peer Support

Peer culture occupies "a critical position in society" (Adler and Adler 2003, 205), and like youths who engage in violent street gang activities, many batterers, rapists, stalkers, and so on are "companions in crime" (Warr 2002). In other words, they are heavily influenced to engage in separation and divorce sexual assault and other variants of woman abuse by their male peers. In fact, a large body of quantitative and qualitative research shows that male peer support is one of the most powerful determinants of such assault.[13] By "male peer support," we mean the multidimensional attachments men form to male peers who themselves sexually assault women, provide resources that perpetuate and legitimate such assaults, or both. There are a variety of sociological and social psychological processes by which peers influence men to sexually victimize women, but the key point here is that such all-male groups encourage, justify, and support the abuse of women by their members. For example, such men provide informational support, that is, guidance and advice that influences men to sexually abuse their partners. Male peer support theory sees such informational support as a motivational factor, allowing men to develop pro-abuse attitudes and behaviors as a result of the encouragement and support of other males, if not of the broader culture at large (Jewkes et al. 2006; Schwartz et al. 2001).

This form of male peer pressure, which legitimizes the sexual objectification of women and the sexual exploitation of them, occurs in all types of cultures throughout the world. For example, William Julius Wilson (1996, 99) found that inner-city African American men were under considerable peer pressure "to be sexually active. They said that the members of their peer networks brag about their encounters and that they feel obligated to reveal their own sexual exploits. Little consideration is given to the implications or consequences of sexual matters for the longer-term relationship."[14]

Far from Wilson's Chicago research site, Campbell found that male drinking practices in rural New Zealand pubs reinforced dominant understandings of legitimate masculine behavior; in this rural area, male pub behavior included men from across the community, making pubs "the key sites for maintaining the legitimacy of hegemonic masculinity in the wider community" (2000, 579). Researchers in both rural and urban parts of other countries (e.g., the United States and England) have uncovered similar data in bars and taverns (Hey 1986; LeMasters 1975; Whitehead 1976). Moreover, as stated earlier, Jewkes et al. (2006) found that nonpartner rapes committed by rural South African men were associated with some male peer support variables, such as criminal gang membership and peer pressure to have sex.

There is also now evidence of the emergence of pro-abuse cyberspace male peer support groups. For example, although the precise number is unknown, exploratory research shows that many men, most of whom probably have never met, share violent pornographic material through e-mail and other electronic channels (DeKeseredy and Schwartz 1998a; Ferguson 1996). These are not innocent users who accidentally come across images, voices, and texts. Nor are they "continually bombarded" with such material against their will. Rather they choose to consume and distribute "cyber porn," and unfortunately, some of these consumers commit lethal acts. Consider this case described by Ian Ferguson (1996, 17):

In late October 1996, the body of a woman from Hampton, Maryland, was pulled from a shallow grave outside the trailer of her lover in Lenoir, North Carolina. The incident occurred shortly after the victim had traveled to Lenoir to meet her lover for the first time following an anonymous e-mail liaison conducted using the pseudonyms "Nancy" and "Slowhand." During this liaison, the two had constructed and participated in several cyber-sexual scenarios involving sado-masochistic practices, torture and snuff. The victim's lover was charged with her murder, but claims that her death was an accident that occurred while the two were living out the sexual fantasies conceived during their e-mail liaison.

Like sexist cultural artifacts used on ritual occasions when male undergraduates gather to affirm their relationships with other men (e.g., life-size inflatable dolls, ice cubes in the shape of nude women), the sharing of cyber porn helps create and maintain sexist male peer groups.[15] Further, this sharing reinforces attitudes that reproduce and reconstitute ideologies of male governance by approvingly presenting women as objects to be conquered and consumed (DeKeseredy and Schwartz 1998a; Jewkes et al. 2006). Future research needs to identify the reasons why men join and participate in such cyber peer groups and how they locate like-minded men. Some rural Ohio men's abusive behavior during or after the process of separation/divorce was associated with group consumption of pornographic material obtained on the Internet, by e-mail, or through other means, as data presented in chapter 4 show.

Most of the work on male peer support theory has been quantitative in nature and conducted on college campuses, as noted earlier, although a few researchers have used qualitative methods to study the relationship between male peer support and various types of woman abuse in urban areas of concentrated disadvantage (Anderson 1999; Bourgois 1995; Wilson 1996).[16] Sinclair (2002) found in a qualitative study that male peer support helped explain woman abuse behavior among socially displaced youth in an eastern Ontario city. Further, DeKeseredy and Schwartz (2002) offer a male peer support theory of woman abuse in public housing, but they did not gather any data specifically on this topic. The topic of interest in this book—sexual assault of women who are breaking up or trying to break up intimate relationships—has been outside the purview of all earlier studies, as for the most part has been the incidence of peer support for sexually aggressive men in rural areas.

Again, the model presented in figure 2.1 theorizes that many patriarchal abusive men have friends who buttress the notion that
woman-initiated separation and divorce threatens men's masculinity.
Furthermore, many members of patriarchal peer groups view wife
beating, rape, and other forms of woman abuse as legitimate and effective means of repairing "damaged patriarchal masculinity" (DeKeseredy
and Schwartz 2005; Messerschmidt 1993; Raphael 2001). Not only do
these men verbally and publicly state that sexual assault and other forms
of abuse are legitimate means of maintaining patriarchal authority and
control, but also they serve as role models, because many of them physically, sexually, and psychologically harm their own intimate partners (see
chapter 4).

An example of a man who used sexual assault as a means of repairing
his damaged masculinity is Jack, Joan's ex-partner, whom she describes
in this episode:

> Um, I began to discuss the idea of him leaving again, um, but I
> wasn't ready to handle the emotional stress of carrying my life plus
> his and what his would do to mine and um, he became, once again,
> very upset. You know me leaving him, me abandoning him. He had
> nowhere to go and no one to be with because he has not contact
> with his family anymore. . . . Um, he accused me of abandoning him
> at a time when he had no one. And, um, I was basically angry at that
> point for what my experiences with him had done to my life, *to my
> life,* and uh, I was basically in the mood of "Well, that's too bad," and
> uh, he wanted to have sex. He said he needed that from me because
> I was making him feel so bad he needed to feel better. And, uh, I told
> him no, that I was just not in the mood to do it and uh, he has very
> large hands, he is much bigger than I am. . . . He pinned both of my
> wrists together and he pinned 'em over my head and continued.

In short, patriarchal male peer support contributes to the perception of damaged masculinity and motivates sexually abusive men to "lash
out against the women . . . they can no longer control" (Bourgois 1995,
214). Another point to consider is that if a patriarchal man's peers see
him as a failure with women because his partner wants to leave or has
left him, he is likely to be ridiculed because he "can't control his
woman." This man has not lived up to his peers' high expectations for

gender-appropriate behavior and therefore must be held accountable (Messerschmidt 1993; Miller 2007; West and Zimmerman 1987). Hence, like many college men who rape women, he is likely to sexually assault his partner to regain status among his peers. Similar to the rapes of female strangers, acquaintances, or dates, the sexual assaults committed by men during or after the process of separation and divorce may have much more to do with their need to sustain their status among their peers than with either a need to satisfy their sexual desires or a longing to regain a loving relationship (Godenzi, Schwartz, and DeKeseredy 2001; Wood and Jewkes 2001).

SUMMARY

Of the very limited theoretical work done so far, our model of separation and divorce sexual assault, presented in figure 2.1, seems the most promising as a building block for future theoretical construction. Obviously, factors besides those included in the model contribute to separation and divorce sexual assault, such as male consumption of pornography (DeKeseredy, Schwartz et al. 2006; Russell 1990, 1998), formal and informal interventions (Ellis and DeKeseredy 1997), and everyday life-events stress (Hardesty 2002). Ours is not a predictive model, and it does not attempt to isolate specific perpetrators; However, several hypotheses derived from it could easily be tested using measures of male peer support developed by DeKeseredy (1988), Smith's (1990) familial patriarchal ideology items, as well as several other measures. Moreover, considerable empirical support for parts of this model appears later on in this book.

We hope that this theory and others, such as one briefly discussed in chapter 6, will be evaluated in the near future using both quantitative and qualitative techniques. The latter are just as important as the former because men are exposed to a wide range of discourses and practices that survey research cannot uncover. To accurately identify and explain how these translate into separation and divorce sexual assault, researchers must "merge into" all-male cultures (Ellen 1984). Moreover, building theories of any type of separation and divorce assault should be "grounded in women's lived experiences," and so far the social scientific research community has not paid enough attention to the words of women who have been victimized by those they have left or want to leave (Hardesty

2002, 618). As Stanko (2006, 546) correctly points out based on her experiences as director of the Economic and Social Research Council Violence Research Program in the United Kingdom: "We had to learn to hear ordinary women about ordinary violence. Now we sometimes listen to what they say. But all too often, in so many areas around the world, we still do not listen enough or effectively. If we did, perhaps we would challenge violence against women—and all violence—more effectively."

In our earlier work, we outlined some of the problems in the state of male peer support theory and the research that needs to be done in the future. Chief among these limitations is the question of whether there are regional variations in male peer support for sexual assault and other types of woman abuse. Recall that there has been very little empirical and theoretical work on men outside the mostly white, mostly middle-class confines of large university campuses—for example, working-class men of the same age in rural communities—to see if their experiences and those of the women they abuse are the same (Jewkes et al. 2006). Further, there has been, to the best of our knowledge, no previous attempt to apply male peer support theory to any type of abuse during separation and divorce sexual assault. Thus, the theory presented in figure 2.1 and the data we describe in chapter 4 constitute attempts to move male peer support research and theorizing beyond the limited realm of academic settings.

CHAPTER 3

The Study

DOING FEMINIST RESEARCH
IN THE HEARTLAND

> While . . . there is no single right way to consult with
> women survivors, their advice contains lessons for
> academics and practitioners alike, including not
> expecting women to participate for free; catering for
> child-care and transportation needs; ensuring that data
> collection does not result in "revictimization" and
> trauma for the women; enabling "safe," equal and
> confidential participation; involving the women in
> decision making about the best means for them to
> participate; not using exclusionary language;
> providing an opportunity for survivors to comment on
> findings at an early stage; and making sure that every
> effort is made so that the findings have a positive
> impact on policy or practice.
>
> —Tina Skinner, Marianne Hester, and Ellen Malos,
> "Methodology, Feminism, and Gender Violence"

IN HER 1997 ARTICLE "Confessions of a Reformed
Positivist: Feminist Participatory Research as Good Social Science,"
University of Dayton sociologist Claire Renzetti, who is widely regarded
as one of the world's leading feminist experts on violence against women,
describes how the undergraduate and graduate research methods courses
she was required to take strongly emphasized the use of "unbiased, objective" techniques of gathering and analyzing quantitative data. She is
definitely not alone, especially in the United States, where positivism
dominates social scientific inquiry.[1] Our own educational experiences,
referred to by some feminist scholars (e.g., Meda Chesney-Lind) as being
restricted to learning "macho methods," are similar to Renzetti's, but we,

too, came to cherish and embrace feminist methods, and we used some of them to gather the qualitative data presented in this book.[2]

For example, we and our research assistants took every effort to adhere to the principles of feminist research outlined in the chapter epigraph. Further, we are among a small number of feminist men who have done qualitative research on violence against women and other sensitive topics (e.g., crime and drug use in public housing) using in-depth interviews (Websdale 2001).[3] Moreover, our respondents' safety was our top priority and we structured the interviews with women to ensure, to the best of our ability, that their ex-partners or others would never find out about these interviews. We cannot emphasize enough that many, if not most, of the women who revealed their violent life experiences to us were at great risk of being killed by the men they left or were trying to leave.[4] Consider, too, that more than half (58 percent) of our interviewees said that the men who hurt them had guns, and some perpetrators had threatened to use them. This is what happened to Ashley when her partner found out that she wanted to leave him:

> And I mean the one night he'd come home and pull a double barrel and cock both barrels and said he was going to kill me. And it was like, wait a minute here, you know, it was two o'clock in the morning. I was sound asleep and I got up at four to go to work. But he'd always keep pressuring me, "If you leave me, I'll find you, I'll kill you. If you leave me, I'll find you, I'll kill you."

Even if women are able to flee to rural shelters, the shelters are seldom effective and rarely safe for women seeking refuge from abuse (Grama 2000). For example, hardly ever is there more than one shelter in a rural town or village, and many people in the community, including abusive men, know exactly where it is. Thus, rural safe houses might be more dangerous than their urban counterparts not only for abused women, but also for the staff, volunteers, and other shelter residents (Fagen 2005).

Ironically, while abused rural women like those who participated in this study experience severe solitude and seclusion, they also lack anonymity in their communities (Fagen 2005).[5] For example, one interviewee said that she refused to tell anyone about her plight because her abuser might hear about it: "But, um, I was at, while this situation was going on I was too afraid to say anything to anybody because I was afraid it would get back to him. And then after it all happened, I didn't want to talk to anybody. I didn't want to hear what anybody had to say."

Regardless of what theoretical or political position one takes or what methods one uses, studying separation/divorce sexual assault involves special challenges in rural communities characterized by geographic and social isolation (Logan et al. 2006; Websdale and Johnson 2005), inadequate (if any) public transportation (Lewis 2003), a powerful good ol' boy network consisting of patriarchal criminal justice officials and some abusive men, and relatively few telephones (Websdale 1998).

In such areas, many abused women live far away from neighbors, other agents of informal social control, social service providers, and criminal justice officials (Fletcher, Lunn, and Reith 1996; Logan et al. 2004; Mahoney, Williams, and West 2001). Websdale's rural Kentucky female respondents told him that their abusers' assaults "feed off of" their partners' isolation. They often use tactics such as destroying their current or ex-wives' cars, which are necessities in rural locations. "Barbara," for example, told Websdale that her ex-husband did not want her to have a car so that she would have to stay with him. In an attempt to get her back, he set her car on fire (Websdale 1998).

Similarly, a woman we interviewed from Meigs County, Ohio, told us, "I didn't have a car. I wasn't allowed to go anywhere." Her husband, however, who had "plenty of cars," disabled them to stop her from seeking freedom and independence: "He would even take the brain off the car, because I figured out how to fix the distributor, so the brain started coming off. Because if you don't have the brain, your car don't start. It was plain and simple. He taught me a lot about cars and I knew what parts I need. And there would be no spare. So, I couldn't leave."

In rural sections of Ohio and other states, as we have seen, there is also widespread acceptance of woman abuse, as well as community norms prohibiting survivors from publicly talking about their experiences and from seeking social support. As this Appalachian Ohio woman we talked to put it: "I don't sit around and share. I keep it to myself. Um, I, I believe that's part of my mental illness. I believe it takes a lot of it. But I'm not one to sit around and talk about what's happened."

Other women we interviewed, such as Emily, were physically forced to keep their abuse a secret from friends, relatives, neighbors, and other people: "I'd be screaming and he would literally put his hands over my mouth because he didn't want his neighbors to know that we were either arguing or fighting and, uh, he got his neighbors believing that it was me, . . . all my fault."

Another respondent told us: "I was only allowed to be around people at work basically. He kept my pretty much to himself. I, like, he even put a stop there for a while, my daughter, I get her for visitation every other weekend, she wasn't even allowed to come and visit at certain times. But I had black and blue marks on me, so you know he didn't want somebody to see that."

Poverty also keeps many rural women from coming into contact with those who can help them or who will listen to their voices. Unable to afford telephones or cars or to take taxis, they suffer in silence. In numerous cases, being economically disadvantaged is not simply the result of the inability to find work in a community plagued by joblessness. It is also a function of separation and divorce (Logan and Walker 2004). This rural Ohio woman provides an example of how leaving an abusive man can cause serious economic hardship:

> I probably went downhill in Chicago like I did. I didn't push for a managerial position because I knew they expected too much of my time and I knew my son was having problems in school and I couldn't find a decent babysitter and it would take up most of my pay anyway. And so and I wasn't getting any child support then and maybe $20 a month if that. And if you break that down that's $5 a week. Hmm, let's see, what can we do with that? That doesn't even pay for lunch, let alone lunch for three days, you know. My kid's always been on the school lunch program, you know. I mean, it's like whatever I've had to do, I don't feel ashamed of doing it. I used to feel ashamed at having to use food stamps. Now it's like it's not my fault that I married someone who's a jackass. And if, you know, this is all the help I can get while he's collecting this and we're on our own, I'm gonna do it, you know. I'm gonna do whatever's best to take care of my child, you know.

We could easily supply an even longer list of problems abused rural women face that also become obstacles for researchers conducting a rural study of separation and divorce sexual assault and other crimes.

However, some of these problems can be overcome or minimized using methods employed in this study.

"Let's Put It in Context": The Research Sites

The subhead of this section is the title of an article written by Bowling Green, Ohio, resident and criminologist Stephen Lab. Although his piece is a commentary on public housing violence research done by Ireland, Thornberry, and Loeber (2003), some of the arguments he raised apply to most social scientific research, including the work described in this book. For example, Lab asserted (2003, 39): "One of the most important things that criminologists often fail to address is the context within which they (their projects or topics) are operating. This is true whether they are proposing a new theory, testing an existing explanation, investigating an emerging phenomenon or evaluating an intervention or program."

What is the broader social, political, and economic context in which we conducted this study based in Appalachia? At first glance, the communities where the women we interviewed lived seem idyllic. Before working full-time at Ohio University from December 2000 to August 2004, Walter DeKeseredy made several trips to southeast Ohio, and he was then, as now, fascinated by the beautiful countryside. His perception is similar to that of many tourists who drive south on Highway 33 and who visit Ohio University's main campus in Athens. However, shortly after he and his family moved to Athens, DeKeseredy became exposed to some major social and economic problems, such as those uncovered by the research reported here and by other social scientists currently or formerly affiliated with Ohio University (e.g. Gilliom 2001; Grant 2008). As stated by an Ohio University student interviewed by Sharon Denham (2005a, 6):

> There is a charm of the backwater towns that I haven't found anywhere else but also a lonely sadness and depressive nature of the people who exist in them. Almost everyone on my father's side of the family (the Appalachian side) has died of some form of cancer and I can't help but think it has something to do with the area. Not to mention the depression and financial needs of such areas. The

suicide rate in these towns is high, and I think it is because not many
see a way out. Although the cultural heritage of this area is rich and
so beautiful, there is a pain and suffering that is still apparent.

Certainly, like the concept "rural," the term "Appalachia" is defined
in many ways. However, it generally refers to a geographic region associated with the Appalachian Mountains and the people who reside there.
Twenty-nine southeast Ohio counties are part of the region designated
in 1965 by the Appalachian Regional Commission (ARC) as part of
Appalachia. Approximately forty-four years ago, President Lyndon
Johnson's administration created the ARC to "fight the war on poverty
in Appalachia" (Denham, 2005c, 5). Still, many southeast Ohio residents
continue to struggle for basic needs such as food and housing. Another
Ohio University student told Denham (2005b, 2):

> I have always lived in Middleport, Ohio. While my community is not
> really considered impoverished, we are what I would consider at an
> economical disadvantage compared to the rest of the state of Ohio.
> Coal mines and power plants have dominated our landscape for
> years. Although the coal mines are gone, the effects are still felt in
> my community. To me, being Appalachian is not just about where
> you live. It also entails culture, lifestyle, and life-outlook. Although
> there are few jobs, our schools seem to be behind (again compared
> to the rest of the state of Ohio), and environmental issues seem to
> be swept under the rug and ignored. I am glad I grew up here and
> continue to live here. In fact, I would not have wanted to live in any
> other place.

Appalachian Ohio's population is approximately 1,455,313; there
are about 101.9 persons per square mile, with an average per capita
personal income of $23,057. The poverty rate is 13.6 percent, at least
twice that of the entire United States. The unemployment rate of 7.1
percent is an underestimate: it does not take into account the people
who have dropped out of the labor force and have stopped looking for
work, often referred to as "discouraged workers" (Alvi, DeKeseredy, and
Ellis 2000). In 2007, 191,502 people in Appalachian Ohio lived at below
poverty level, and 12.3 percent of the population had college degrees
(Appalachian Regional Commission 2007b). In light of these data, it is

not surprising that the Appalachian Regional Commission defines our respondents' communities as economically distressed; the ARC predicts for the entire Appalachian region the following challenges (2007a, 1):

- The region faces competition from imports in key industries, such as textiles and apparel manufacturing.
- In counties where manufacturing remains a dominant industry, declining real wages have eroded the income base. Moreover, high-wage, high-tech jobs have not developed in these manufacturing-dependent counties. The result is a widening income gap between these counties and the faster growing metropolitan counties where information services are concentrated.
- In many central Appalachian counties, the economic decline of the coal industry has contributed to their continued distress. Even with an anticipated rise in coal prices, the business and employment base of these counties is still expected to decline.
- Seventy-one distressed counties still have a high dependence on tobacco production. This poses another threat to the economy of the most vulnerable parts of the region.

Appalachian Ohio, along with other parts of the United States, also faces the "Wal-Marting of rural America" and its damaging effects on local businesses (Tunnell 2006). Due in large part to Wal-Mart's annual average of more than two hundred new store openings, many local rural stores cannot compete and must close down (Stone 1997). Wal-Mart's response? "The small business is going to have to adjust" (Davidson 1996, 49–50). Some more indicators of a crisis in Appalachian Ohio and other rural U.S. communities are "abandoned farm houses, idle farm machinery, illegal trash dumping, methamphetamine manufacturing, and OxyContin diversion" (Tunnell 2006, 335; Weisheit and Kernes 2003).

Although certainly not all Appalachian Ohio women endure serious hardships, Lisa Contos Shoaf's (2004, 1) conclusions from a rural Ohio study she conducted in 2003 by now sound familiar to us:

The culture and tradition in Appalachia can influence the level of intervention, support, and protection given to battered women. Traditionally, Appalachian culture views domestic violence as a family matter, not as a serious crime, thus discouraging victims from seeking help. This culture also generally reinforces traditional male/female roles, such as the role of the male as head of the household. This can impact the woman's ability to seek help and it can impact her ability to receive help from others who may also subscribe to this patriarchal ideology. Victim support can be further complicated by familiarity among community members, as those who report incidents of domestic violence tend to be stigmatized within these smaller communities. Furthermore, issues may be handled differently when the law enforcement or prosecutors know the abusers, as the criminal justice response to the abusive incident may be minimized. Cultural traits also impact prosecutorial efforts. For example, Appalachian culture emphasizes hunting as a favorite pastime. Under federal law, a convicted domestic violence abuser loses his right to own or possess a gun if convicted, a factor which may influence whether the abuser will plead guilty to a domestic violence charge.

Our sexual assault study uncovered similar findings. It is to the first step we took to develop the Appalachian Ohio study reported here that we turn to first.

PREPARATORY RESEARCH

To design a study that effectively and sensitively addressed the complexities of separation and divorce in rural Ohio communities, the research team included a "preparatory component of qualitative investigation" (MacLean 1996). This involved several meetings, e-mail exchanges, and in-depth telephone conversations with leading researchers in the field, local battered women's shelter staff, sexual assault survivor advocates, police officers, mental health workers, and others with a vested interest in curbing the pain and suffering uncovered by this research.[6] Not only did these people strongly support the study, but also they sensitized the research team to key issues not addressed in the social scientific literature on separation and divorce sexual assault, such as the influence of broader Ohio state politics. Moreover, they made several major contributions to the development of highly useful screening questions (see appendix A) and a semi-structured interview schedule (see appendix B). As Schechter (1988, 311) notes, activists and practitioners are experts on woman abuse and "can help researchers formulate sophisticated and intellectually rich questions."[7] Further, they put us into contact with service providers and criminal justice officials throughout Ohio, such as those affiliated with the Ohio Domestic Violence Network and the Ohio Coalition Against Sexual Assault. Practitioners also referred to us six of the forty-three women who participated in this study.

The research team explicitly, sincerely, and publicly acknowledged that service providers are experts on woman abuse, following Schechter (1988) and other feminist scholars. Further, we routinely shared our findings with all the practitioners who helped craft this study, and both authors served on the board of directors of an Athens, Ohio, shelter. Walter DeKeseredy also became an active member of the Athens County Coalition Against Sexual Assault during the data-gathering phase of the project, and he is still a member of the Ohio Domestic Violence Network Advisory Board. Furthermore, since DeKeseredy was a member of the California Coalition Against Sexual Assault's (CALCASA) Campus Advisory Board, he was able to seek valuable advice and guidance from CALCASA executives such as Sandy Ortman and continues to do so.

SAMPLE SELECTION AND RECRUITMENT

Data on the relationship between separation and divorce and nonlethal forms of woman abuse such as beatings have been primarily derived from surveys. But simply establishing through statistical means that separated and divorced women report higher rates of violence than do their married and cohabiting counterparts does not reveal whether abuse caused the termination of relationships or if it started during or after breakups (Block and DeKeseredy 2007). Still, we know that the connection between separation and divorce and woman abuse is much more than a coincidence (Hardesty 2002). To infer causality, however, requires other research methods. This is not to say that survey methods are not valuable means of collecting data on problems identified in this book and elsewhere. The point, rather, is that to develop a richer understanding of these issues it is necessary to listen to women's voices, because this "may be the only way to describe a complex reality for which we have few names" (Mahoney 1991, 41). Further, as Danielle Fagen discovered during the course of helping us gather the qualitative data presented throughout this book (2005, 40):

> Face-to-face interviews help eliminate the possibility of misunderstandings, by allowing the researcher to condense and interpret the meaning of what the participant is talking about and "send" it back to the participant. Then, the participant can reply either "Yes, this is what I was talking about" or "No. I didn't mean that." Problems with illiteracy can also be countered through interviewing.

Another important feature of the qualitative methods we used is that, as Keith Davis (2006, xiv) puts it, "we can see women who are resilient and who have come through a version of hell by coping effectively with . . . horrible experiences." Still, the same obstacles researchers encounter in their attempts to do face-to-face interviews with rural women present themselves in any attempt to gain access in a telephone or self-report survey (Weisheit, Falcone, and Wells 2006). Therefore, techniques like those employed by Lee Bowker (1983) and by Logan et al. (2006) to collect data on various types of woman abuse in other parts of the United States generated the sample. For example, we placed an advertisement once a week during two different six-week periods in a free newspaper available throughout Athens County, Ohio (see box 3.1). Also, we pinned up posters about the study in public places such as courthouses and gave them to social service providers who come into contact with abused women.

In addition:

Two local newspapers gave considerable coverage to the project.

Ohio University sent out a press release to newspapers and other Ohio-based media.

Three local radio stations and Ohio University's television station carried public service announcements about the study.

The director of a local shelter and Walter DeKeseredy appeared on a local television news show to discuss this project and broader issues related to it.

3.1 NEWSPAPER ADVERTISEMENT

Call for interested women of Athens, Hocking, and Vinton Counties for participation in an Ohio University research project

Have you ever had unwanted sexual experiences while trying to leave your husband or male live-in partner?

Or, have you ever had unwanted sexual experiences after you left your husband or male live-in partner?

We would greatly appreciate your participation in a confidential interview. Your name will not be given to anyone.

We will pay you $25.00 for your time and transportation costs. Also, we will talk to you at a time and location of your choosing.

If you would like to be interviewed, please call Mae at (xxx) xxx–xxxx or Carolyn at (xxx) xxx–xxxx.

The Ohio Domestic Violence Network and other agencies told interested parties (e.g., rural shelter workers) about the study and helped recruit participants.

Local shelter staff, a police department social worker, employees of the county sheriff's department, Planned Parenthood, Women's Center staff at a local two-year college, and employees of the local Sexual Assault Survivor Advocate Program informed possible respondents about the study.

Sociologist Judith Grant, then at Ohio University, told women who participated in her addiction study about the research.[8]

Indexlike cards with the information provided in the recruiting poster were routinely placed on top of newspaper boxes, both inside stores and on sidewalks in Athens, Ohio.

INTERVIEWING PROCEDURES

With the assistance of Judith Grant, Walter DeKeseredy taught the research assistants selected to conduct interviews with great care to ensure that they infused a sense of "trust, safety, and intimacy" into the interviewing process (Brush 1990; Russell 1990; Smith 1994).[9] Similar to the approach taken by Russell (1990) in the development of her marital rape survey, the training included "consciousness raising" about sexual assault and the "defining and desensitizing" of sexual words to make the interviewers as comfortable as possible with whatever language respondents might use (Smith 1994). The local shelter staff and Walter DeKeseredy also sensitized interviewers to the dominant norms and values of the people who reside in rural sections of Ohio.

Concrete examples of the training techniques include:[10]

- In-depth briefings on the nature and purpose of the study, the gender sensitive issues involved, and ways of handling potential emergency situations (e.g., if a respondent experiences traumatic memories).

- Engagement by the interviewers in a series of mock interviews under the supervision of Judith Grant and Walter DeKeseredy to identify and correct difficulties.

- Discussions of appropriate nonverbal communication (e.g., nonjudgmental body language) to be used in the interview situation.

From early March 2003 until early April 2004, two female research assistants carried cellular phones twenty-four hours a day to receive calls from women interested in participating in the study. They told callers the purpose of the study and then asked a series of screening questions to determine their eligibility to be interviewed. The main criteria were age (eighteen or older) and having ever had any type of unwanted sexual experience when they wanted to end, were trying to end, or had ended a relationship with a husband or live-in male partner.[11] We invited each woman who met the selection criteria to a semi-structured face-to-face interview at a time and place of her choosing.

At the start of these interviews, we again told women the purpose of the study and asked them to sign a consent form. We also reminded them that the interview would be highly confidential, that they could end the interview at any time, and that they did not have to answer any of the questions (appendix B). After the interview, the women received $25.00 for their time and $7.75 for travel expenses, along with an index card listing the locations and phone numbers of local support services for survivors.[12] (Index or palm cards are much safer than sheets of paper because they minimize the likelihood of abusive ex-partners and others, such as ex-partners' male friends, discovering that respondents spoke with others of their abusive experiences.) We also invited interviewees to contact the research team at a later time if they had questions or concerns. Although the team was deeply committed to generating rich qualitative data, it was more concerned with ensuring respondents' safety in communities where most residents know each other.

We conducted six interviews over the phone, five off campus in safe places selected by respondents, and the rest in an Ohio University office.[13] Most of the participants who came to the campus did not tell us how they got there, but the research team assumed that friends or relatives drove them. None of the participants disclosed how they had access to telephones. It is reasonable to conclude that they felt revealing such information would jeopardize their safety.

Research assistants tape-recorded and transcribed the interviews, most of which lasted about ninety minutes. Forty-three women participated in this study. Posters placed in public places attracted most of our respondents (twenty-seven). Eight women called after exposure to ads or media stories about the study, and individuals or organizations referred eight other women to the research team. Most respondents—thirty of the forty-three—lived in Athens County, Ohio; three lived in Hocking County, Ohio; one lived in Vinton County, Ohio; and nine lived in other rural parts of the state. The mean age of the sample was thirty-five, and the mean income for 2002 was $13,588. Twenty-eight (65 percent) had some postsecondary education. Close to half the participants were unemployed. Of the twenty-five who had been married, all were divorced or legally separated, but only five remarried. Most of our respondents had children, and the research team provided child care for two interviewees.[14]

SUMMARY

Similar to what Bowker (1983) found when he tried to conduct a woman abuse study in Racine, Wisconsin, many rural Ohio women strongly adhere to privacy norms and have little faith that survey researchers can guarantee their promise of confidentiality, especially those who are "outsiders" not from the community (Lewis 2003).[15] For these and other reasons, feminist means of gathering qualitative data on rural separation and divorce sexual assault are necessary. The methods we selected are by no means unorthodox; the sample selection techniques are similar to those used by Bowker (1983) to recruit Milwaukee women who have successfully "beaten wife-beating" and to procedures used by DeKeseredy et al. (2003) to recruit participants in their Canadian study of poverty and crime in public housing. These methods are also similar to those used by Logan et al. (2006) to recruit female victims of stalking in both rural and urban communities.

Methodological improvements are needed in future studies (see chapter 6 for suggestions for further empirical work). We hope the data reported in chapters 4 and 5 will motivate others to pursue these recommendations or use other approaches that may be just as good or better. Much more research needs to be done in this arena, and the behaviors described in chapters 4 and 5 constitute just the tip of the iceberg.

CHAPTER 4

Exiting Dangerous Relationships

RURAL WOMEN'S EXPERIENCES
OF ABUSE AND RISK FACTORS

He wanted me to have sex with a few people. Okay,
like I was telling you earlier, and I didn't want to. And,
uh, I finally did. And then I got beat for it because I
did. I tried not to, but then when we did, I got beat.
And that's not good. And then, we was at one of his
friend's house and we got drunk and I fell off a four-
foot-drop porch and I remember, I don't remember
how I got off the porch, but I remember being put in
the car and going home. I remember being put in the
bed, with all my clothes on. But when I woke up,
everything was off but my shirt. And I asked my
husband, "Did you have sex with me last night?" He
said, "Yep, while you were passed out." I said, "What
encouraged you to sleep with anybody who can't even
move?" He replied, "Oh, all I had to do was hold your
legs for you."

Nickie, rural Ohio interviewee

BASED ON THEIR ANALYSIS OF DATA generated by the
first U.S. National Family Violence Survey, Murray Straus, Richard Gelles,
and Suzanne Steinmetz (1981, 32) argued that the "marriage license is a
hitting license." Their thesis includes two contentions: (1) marriage is a
special institution that places women at high risk of being physically
assaulted by their husbands, and (2) married women are more likely to be
beaten than are unmarried women. If we accept their argument, then the
logical solution to wife abuse and other forms of male-to-female victimization is for these women to exit their relationships. If they were no

longer married, they would no longer be beaten. One thing we know, as mentioned earlier, is that most women leave violent relationships. Others have remarked on this same phenomenon (e.g., Block 2003; Logan and Walker 2004). Nevertheless, data presented in this chapter support the conclusion that, for many women, separation or divorce does not improve their quality of life. In fact, exiting can exacerbate their pain and suffering. What makes the findings presented in this chapter unique is that they reflect the abusive experiences of rural women who receive relatively little attention from the research community.

TYPES AND TIMING OF ABUSE

Chapter 1 lists the definitions of the four types of sexual assault used in this study. The number of respondents who ever experienced one or more of these behaviors is presented in table 4.1. Only a few of the forty-three women experienced just one of these forms of separation or divorce sexual assault, and virtually all experienced rape or attempted rape. "Blackmail rapes" are not uncommon, as we have said. For example, Tina wanted to leave her partner but was afraid of losing her children. Asked why her partner sexually assaulted her, she replied:

> Um, to punish me for leaving him. To punish me for getting pregnant, um, to punish me for embarrassing him, and um, to control me. . . . And then something would happen and he would know it was getting close to the end of our relationship once again and he would start it. And the whole time I would be crying, but I couldn't cry loud enough because if his parents heard us he swore he would take our children away. I know he did this when he thought I was getting ready to leave, and he knew that I couldn't live without my children.

TABLE 4.1
Separation and Divorce Sexual Assault Prevalence Rates (N = 43)

Type of Sexual Assault	N	%
Sexual contact	19	44
Sexual coercion	32	74
Attempted rape	8	18
Rape	35	81

TABLE 4.2
Nonsexual Abuse Prevalence Rates (N = 43)

Type of Nonsexual Abuse	N	%
Physical violence	36	84
Psychological abuse	38	88
Economic abuse	30	70
Abuse of pets	5	12
Stalking	16	37
Destruction of prized possessions	22	51

Regardless of the nature or the type of relationship they have with men, women targeted for intimate violence are rarely victimized by only one form of abuse. Rather, they typically suffer from a variety of injurious behaviors that include sexual assault, physical violence, psychological abuse, economic blackmail or denying them money even if they earn wages, harm to animals or possessions to which they have attachments, or stalking behavior (Logan et al. 2006).[1] Most (80 percent) of the women we interviewed were victimized by two or more of these forms of abuse. The rates they reported are presented in table 4.2, where each different type of abuse is counted once, but a single person can be counted in more than one category.

Joan was among the woman harmed by various types of abuse during the process of exiting a relationship:

> Well, what happened was that he got drunk and wanted sex from me and I told him no. I said, "Stay away from me. I can't stand you when you're drinking. Get away from me." He started grabbing my butt, and playing with my legs, and trying to grab my boobs. And everything, anything to get what he wanted. And I told him, I kicked him in the leg, and I told him, "Get away from me." And then got into a fight over it and then he started throwing stuff at my face and I went to the phone and I said, "I'm gonna call your probation officer." I says, "If you don't leave me alone and you've been drinking, you're acting like an ass. Leave me the hell alone." And he wouldn't. He unplugged the phone. I plugged it in, I plugged it, you know. It was back and forth. He unplugged, I plugged it in. He unplugged it, I

plugged it in; . . . when he was trying to prevent me from getting the phone, he stepped on my foot, which fractured the top of my foot. I was on crutches for two weeks.

In addition to being sexual assaulted, an Athens County, Ohio, woman also experienced other types of abuse after her partner discovered that she wanted to leave him. "Yes, um, he was abusive," she said. "He was very emotionally abusive. He liked to put me down. He used to tell me"—she took a deep breath—"that I was a horrible mother, that he was going to take my kids away from me, that I was, you know, a horrible person, that I was stupid. He used to shove me up against walls and choked me all the times."

Most victims of separation and divorce sexual assault are also hurt by other highly injurious acts (see table 4.2). And sometimes they are not the only ones injured by ex-partners, as stated earlier. For example, 19 percent of the respondents stated that their partners abused their children, and one woman believes that her ex-partner raped her to kill her unborn child.[2] Trina spoke of her ex-husband: "He came back October of the same year for a so-called emergency visitation, and he was able to take my daughter away from me for eight hours even though the DNA had never been proven. And when my daughter finally came back, she had severe diaper rash, smelled like cigarettes and alcohol, and had bruises right, right on her thighs and on her wrists."

We interviewed one woman who was coerced by her husband into having an abortion, on top of repeatedly being forced to have children when she didn't want to:

> I feel humiliated for having been there all those years, but I didn't want to be. I just didn't know what to do. I have five children. I shouldn't have had any. I was pregnant ten times. One of the pregnancies ended in abortion. I actually went to the doctor and had an abortion on purpose. The other ones were miscarriages. I don't believe in abortion. I didn't believe in abortion at the time. I had never believed in it in my life. I figured there are better ways. And yet I had one because not only did he first get me pregnant when I didn't want to be pregnant, but he told me that he would leave and I would be left alone if I didn't do something about the baby. I

remember that all the time. I've done things that go against my personal moral standards.... Another thing is he was constantly degrading me, telling me that I did a terrible job at sex, and I'm thinking,
Then why don't you go away and find somebody else?

A few women in our sample will never be able to have children
because their reproductive organs were damaged by numerous sexual
assaults committed by their former husbands or common-law partners, a
circumstance of which this woman spoke:

> My biggest concern right now is that I recently found out that I
> will not be able to carry children. So I guess my biggest concern
> right now is finding a way to convince my boyfriend that it's going
> to be all right, kind of keeping my relationship together, you know.
> He, he's [abusive ex-partner] not a concern anymore because he's
> gone and he's been gone for a while. And school's not really a con-
> cern and work's not really a concern. It's that, that's like a major, it
> had a major impact on my life. I didn't want to have kids until I got
> pregnant. And then I get pregnant and I lose my kid, and now, I'm
> like, damn! You know, I wanted to be a mom. And then they tell
> you, you can't have them again, period, and that's kind of messing
> with me.

Some men did not hit their children or force them to have sex but
behaved in other ways that are sexually and psychologically abusive. In
one instance, a man exposed children to pornography shortly after he
realized that his wife was going to leave him. "I walked in to him mas-
turbating in front of my children to *Penthouse*," she said. And "there were
naked pictures, well, not naked, but pictures of me in a bra and underwear that he had stolen and had developed."

When is the most likely time for separation or divorce sexual assault
to occur? As other studies discovered (e.g., Sev'er 1997), it may be when
a woman expresses a desire to leave a relationship. Of the women in our
study, thirty-two (74 percent) were sexually assaulted at that time.
Twenty-one (49 percent) were sexually abused while they were trying to
leave or while they were leaving, and fourteen (33 percent) were victimized after they left. Obviously, many of these women were victimized
at two or more of these times.

Although it is difficult to make hard comparisons from small numbers, there is no question that in this sample, formerly married women
reported a higher rate of sexual assault at each stage than did cohabiting
women. For example, compared to cohabiting women (six, or 33 percent), married women (twelve, or 47 percent) were more likely to report
being abused while still in the relationship, before expressing a desire to
exit, trying to exit, or exiting their relationships. At the next stage, when
the women reported that they wanted to leave their abusive relationship,
twenty of the twenty-five married women (80 percent) stated that they
were sexually assaulted, while twelve of the eighteen cohabiting women
(67 percent) said that their assaults occurred at this juncture. These marital status variations data may be the result of married men perceiving
greater threats to their sense of entitlement and a stronger adherence to
the belief that their wives are their property (Bergen 1996, 2006; Frieze
1983). As one wife rapist said to Finkelhor and Yllo (1985, 72), "When
she would not give it freely . . . I would take it. That's as honest as I can
get." He told Finkelhor and Yllo, but not his wife, that when she rejected
his sexual advances, it made him angry and made him think, "You can't
deny me. I have a right to this. You're not satisfying my needs."

In sum, many survivors of separation and divorce sexual assault
experienced other forms of abuse. Thus, separation and divorce sexual
assault is multidimensional in nature. The most likely time for sexual
assault to occur is when a woman expresses a desire to exit a relationship. Since we gleaned these reported results from a small nonrepresen-
tative sample, we cannot generalize from them to any larger rural sample
or population. Still, these findings strongly suggest that separation and
divorce sexual assault is a major social problem in rural parts of Ohio at
least, and these data challenge the notion that rural areas are at low risk
for violent crime.

CHARACTERISTICS OF MEN WHO SEXUALLY ASSAULTED THEIR EX-PARTNERS

Male Peer Support

Again, male peer support refers to "the attachments to male peers
and the resources they provide which encourage and legitimate woman
abuse" (DeKeseredy 1990, 130). It is not surprising that this factor was a
constant theme among our respondents' stories, given that it is strongly

associated with other types of woman abuse, such as date rape, campus party rape, nonpartner rape in rural South Africa, and wife beating (Armstrong, Hamilton, and Sweeney 2006; Bowker 1983; DeKeseredy and Schwartz, 1998b, 2002; Jewkes et al. 2006). Twenty-nine (67 percent) of the interviewees reported on a variety of ways in which their part- ners' male peers perpetuated and legitimated separation and divorce sex- ual assault.

Three methods in particular stand out: frequently drinking with male friends, informational support, and attachment to abusive peers. Informational support refers to the guidance and advice that influences men to sexually, physically, and psychologically abuse their female part- ners, and attachment to abusive peers is defined as having male friends who also abuse women (DeKeseredy 1988). These factors are identical to those found to be highly significant in predicting which men on college campuses will admit to being sexual predators (DeKeseredy and Schwartz, 1998b; Schwartz et al. 2001).

Frequent drinking with friends is often associated with the develop- ment of a particular kind of masculinity that objectifies women and endorses male behavior that can be physically and sexually violent (Campbell 2000; DeKeseredy and Schwartz 2005). Thirty-three (77 per- cent) of the women in our study said that their former partners fre- quently drank alcohol, and twenty-seven (63 percent) said their partners spent large amounts of time with their male friends and most of the time spent together involved drinking alcohol.[3] Further, as is the case with college men who sexually abuse women, "nights out drinking with the boys" were seen by many respondents as contexts that often supported patriarchal conversations about women and how to control them.[4] As Susan reported: "Um, they're basically like him. They sit around, talk about women, and gossip. They're the biggest gossips there ever was. But they sit around and brag how many times they get it and how they keep their women in line and, you know, just like crap, you know."

The social settings Susan and other respondents described are also examples of the factor of informational support, although these were not restricted to group drinking events. For example, one respondent's abu- sive partner spent much time with his cousin, a man who "hated women" and who often called them "fuckin' bitches" and "whore sluts." Her partner also had a married brother who "hit his wife every so often."

Another woman said that her ex-partner's friends "love to put women in the ground. Women are nothing but dirt." Although most of the participants did not explicitly label their partners' peers as patriarchal, most of them are, for, as Lynn stated, "they just think women are their property and they can lay 'em anytime they want to. That's just their whole attitude about it." Twenty of the women interviewed (47 percent) said that they knew their partners' friends also physically or sexually abused women, which indicates that attachment to abusive peers also contributes to separation and divorce assault. In fact, Betty told us that *all* her ex-partners' friends hit women or sexually assault them, and several women told us that they directly observed their partners' friends abusing female intimates. Jackie is one such participant: "I watched a friend of his who shoved a friend of mine up against a wall . . . and try to, you know, have his way with her."

A few perpetrators also enlisted the help of their friends to sexually abuse some of the women in our study. Such male peer support frequently involved forcing women to have sex with friends, which is what happened to Marie:

> Well, him and his friend got me so wasted. They took turns with me and I remembered most of it, but, um, there was also drugs involved. Not as much on my behalf as theirs. I was just drunk. And I did remember most of it, and the next morning I woke up feeling so dirty and so degraded and then it ended up getting around that I was the slut. . . . And in my eyes that was rape, due to the fact that I was so drunk. And I definitely didn't deserve that. And I was hurting. I was hurting the next day.

This incident is similar to what Peggy Reeves Sanday (1990) uncovered in her study of fraternity gang rape: in groups, some men do not rely on force to have sex with women but use alcohol or drugs to "work a yes" out of them (see box 4.1). In other words, some perpetrators, either alone or in a group, purposely get women so drunk that they cannot resist their advances (Armstrong, Hamilton, and Sweeney 2006), which is a form of felony forcible rape in Ohio and most other states. Nevertheless, it is unlikely that the criminal justice authorities will prosecute any male who rapes a woman under these conditions. Few people in the criminal justice system even consider it a crime to forcibly rape an intimate partner or acquaintance under any circumstance (DeKeseredy, Ellis, and Alvi 2005; Harney and Muehlenhard 1991). It is a difficult task to convince men that it is wrong to rape, when not only their male peers sanction or reward such behavior but also members of the general public point out that the woman was drunk and therefore responsible for her own rape.

Interestingly, few people would suggest that a woman who passes out from alcohol consumption in a bar shares the responsibility for having her jacket or purse stolen, nor would many argue against prosecuting the thief. Furthermore, if we knew that the thief had encouraged the victim to drink more so that she would not be able to resist the theft of her jacket and purse, we would be even more outraged. However, when sex is involved, people often see the facts as ambiguous and the moral

---

4.1 "Working a Yes Out"

It was her first fraternity party. The beer flowed freely and she had much more to drink than she had planned. It was hot and crowded and the party spread out all over the house, so that when three men asked her to go upstairs, she went with them. They took her into a bedroom, locked the door and began to undress her. Groggy with alcohol, her feeble protests were ignored as the three men raped her. When they finished, they put her in the hallway, naked, locking her clothes in the bedroom. (Small eastern liberal arts college)

A nineteen-year-old woman student was out on a date with her boyfriend and another couple. They were all drinking beer and after going back to the boyfriend's dorm room, they smoked two marijuana cigarettes. The other couple left and the woman and her boyfriend had sex. The woman fell asleep and the next thing she knew she awoke with a man she didn't know on top of her trying to force her into having sex. A witness said the man was in the hall with two other men when the woman's boyfriend came out of his room and invited them to have sex with his unconscious girlfriend. (Small midwestern college)

Source: Sanday (1990, 3) took these examples
from Ehrhart and Sandler 1985.

waters as muddied (Fenstermaker 1989). Nor is it only in fairly minor cases that people are confused about blame and morality and therefore award men immunity from punishment; even in serious cases such as gang rape, there will be no serious punishment in most communities (Schwartz and DeKeseredy 1997).

Although the following incident did not involve male peer support, it is another glaring example of using alcohol as a means of "working a yes out," as Carrie reports:

> I agreed to meet with him to discuss visitation and child support for our daughter, and I wanted to go to a public place after everything he had done because it wasn't just sexual, it was mental, physical. And I showed up there. I had a couple of friends who were sitting throughout keeping an eye on me. Ordered the drink, got up to use the bathroom, drank my drink, and that was pretty much the last thing I remembered until the next morning when I woke up with a killer headache and my daughter crying in her crib. . . . He was in bed next to me. . . . I had strangulation marks around my neck. I had marks around my wrists and an open wound on my face, and he had obviously had sex.

A few women forced to have group sex were also beaten after going through brutal degradation experiences. This is what happened to Janet:

> He ended up bringing someone into the relationship, which I didn't want, but he told me that if I didn't do it he would leave me. And I ended up staying with him. He was more into group sex and, and uh trying to be the big man. He wanted sex in a group thing or with his buddies or made me have sex with a friend of his. See, one time he made me have sex with a friend of his for him to watch, and then he got mad and hit me afterwards. I mean, he tied me up so I could watch him have sex with a thirteen-year-old girl. And then he ended up going to prison for it. So, I mean, it was nasty.

Lorraine recalled an incident that occurred during the end of her relationship: "He wanted me to have sex with a few people. Okay, like I was telling you earlier, and I didn't want to. . . . And, uh, I finally did. And then I got beat for it because I did. I tried not to, but then when we did, I got beat."

The kind of gang rape uncovered by our study is often referred to as "streamlining" in South Africa and is, according to Jewkes et al. (2006, 2951),

> essentially a rape by two or more perpetrators. It is an unambiguously defiling and humiliating act, and is often a punishment, yet at the same time it is an act that is often regarded by its perpetrators as rooted in a sense of entitlement (Wood 2005). A woman may be streamlined to punish her for having another partner; for behaving outside gender norms (e.g., when deeply intoxicated) (Wojcicki 2002); for being successful, or for imagining she could be superior. Streamlining is sometimes an act of male bonding, a "favor" to the boyfriend's friends. (Niehaus 2005; Wood 2005)

Patriarchal Control

Seventy-nine percent of the women in our study said that their partners strongly believed that men should be in charge and control of domestic household settings. For example, Marie said that her ex-husband "wanted to be in control. He was in control for us, or you know I felt it." Similarly, Rita told us that her ex-partner "was the type of person where women were lower than men. And men were able, you know—women had to do what men told them. Which is pretty much my whole relationship with him."

Like Joan's ex-husband, many of the interviewees' partners isolated them to maintain control. "He didn't allow me to socialize at all," Joan said. "My place was at home with the children, and that's where I was most of the time. The only thing I went out for was if they had a parent-teacher conference at school. I went for that. But no, I had no outside contact." Until she left him, another respondent's partner made it clear where he thought she belonged: "His favorite thing was, 'If you are not going to be at work, you're going to be here cooking and cleaning, doing laundry. And if I ever catch you sitting on your ass, I am going to beat the fuck out of you, you know.'"

Most respondents said they were raped during or after separation and divorce because their partners wanted to show them "who was in charge." Tanya was one of many interviewees who had a partner determined not to let her go:

He did it because I was his and he felt he could. And it was his way of letting me know that, ah, first of all, of letting me know that I was his. And secondly, letting me know that um, that I wasn't safe anywhere. And I, when we were together, when he had forced me to go back together with him, ah, he, ah . . . raped me as another form of, of possession. And I think also as a reminder of what could happen. And ultimately, at one point, I believed that he raped me as part of his means of killing my unborn child.

Nickie had similar experiences:

I was his property that he wanted to own me. And I was his. That's how he looked at it. I was his property, and that's all that I felt I was to him, was just a lay, you know. But that's all he wanted me for was to satisfy himself. . . . He would deprive me. It was more of a mental torture, emotionally, mental torture than physical except in the sex it was physical. "You're mine and I'm gonna have you whether you want it or not. I want you." He was in control. And that's what it's all about with men like that. They have to be in control.

Another woman identified the same motive: "I think it was probably him sensing, you know, that it was just about to end, that I couldn't take it anymore. You know, so because, uh, there was meanness there. It was, you know, it was a control thing. I didn't really look at him as a controlling person at the time, even throughout our whole relationship, but, uh, I think I was really deceived by that."

That close to 80 percent of the men who abused their partners—the women in this study—adhered to the ideology of familial or societal patriarchy may also partly explain why so many of them had peers who were sexist or abusive. DeKeseredy and Schwartz (1998b) uncovered a strong statistical relationship between Canadian college men's patriarchal attitudes and beliefs and their affiliations with male peers who perpetuate and legitimate physical, sexual, and psychological abuse in dating relationships. More specifically, these researchers found that Canadian college men who report abusing their girlfriends and dating partners are more likely than those who do not report abusive behavior to endorse an ideology of familial patriarchy. They also found that these men are even more likely to be abusive if male peers support their sexist ideology and injurious behaviors.

What follows is one example of how male peers supported what they saw as an interviewee's husband's right to maintain his patriarchal control with abuse. This incident happened shortly after the woman's husband found out that she wanted to leave him: "I remember my husband making me have sex with him one time when people were in the next room, and none of them guys would come in and help me. And they knew he was hitting me, but they figured that he was my husband. If it were a stranger, it would have been different."

Did male peers teach interviewees' partners to engage in separation and divorce sexual assault, or did abusive men seek the friendship and support of violent peers? These are important empirical questions that can be answered only empirically. Future research on separation and divorce sexual assault, we hope, will be specifically designed to uncover data on the complex relationship between patriarchy, male peer support, and the abuse uncovered by this study.

Pornography

Today, pornography is, as Rus Funk (2006, 163) puts it,

> a huge industry. One measure of its size is by annual sales. In 1997, the estimated amount of money spent on pornography was $4.2 billion a year; as of 2000, the revenue of the U.S. pornography industry was estimated at $12 billion. This is more money than the annual sales of baseball, movies, and music combined. It is estimated that there are well over a million so-called sex sites on the Internet, with as many as 10,000 being added every week.[5]

In addition to having a major financial impact, pornography, many feminists contend, is strongly associated with various types of violence against women (Bergen and Bogle 2000; R. Jensen 2007). A few studies have found that the contribution of pornography to woman abuse in dating is related to male peer support (DeKeseredy and Schwartz 1998b; Schwartz and DeKeseredy 1998). Some men learn to sexually objectify women through their exposure to pornographic media (Funk 2006; R.

Jensen 1995), and they often learn these lessons in groups, such as pornographic film showings at fraternity houses (Sanday 1990).

Such "strengthening" of male "misogynist bonds" is not a recent phenomenon (Lehman 2006). For example, as Linda Williams (1999) and other film scholars have noted, cinematic pornography originated in 16 mm silent films, which were "usually shown in private all-male 'smokers' in such contexts as bachelor parties and the like. Within such a context, the men laughed and joked and talked among themselves while watching the sexually explicit films about women, who though absent from the audience, were the likely butt of the jokes, laughing, and rude remarks" (Lehman 2006, 4).

Similarly, some rural survivors of separation and divorce sexual assault said that their partners consumed pornography with their male friends while drinking excessive amounts of alcohol. Agnes, one interviewee who experienced this problem, described this episode: "They were drinking and carrying on and they had, um, they had a bunch of porno stuff in the garage, and I had walked in and I had started to tear it up. And I was, I was, I thought it was gross. I was mad at it. I was mad at him for being around it. And he just started charging after me, and I started running to my car as fast as I could. And he got into the car and he threw me down in the seat and he just kept punching me, punching me."

Regardless of whether they consumed it in groups, 65 percent of the estranged partners of the women in our study viewed pornography, and 30 percent of the interviewees reported that pornography was involved in sexually abusive events they experienced.[6] This figure supports Robert Jensen's (2007) finding that some violent men use "pornography as a training manual for abuse" (Bergen and Bogle 2000, 231). Thus, some of the men who abused our respondents may be graduates of what Lundy Bancroft (2002, 185) refers to as "the Pornography School of Sexuality."

Does pornography cause separation and divorce sexual assault and other forms of woman abuse? The data generated by this study cannot answer this question; finding the answer requires a long-term and expensive longitudinal research design. Generally, there are some important competing arguments. For example, for men who physically and sexually abuse women, pornography may well be just one more weapon in their arsenal. Hence, a man who cares that his partner would be scared or

angry might not expose her to the lessons he learned from a pornographic movie, while his abusive friend might try to force his estranged
partner to act out such scenes over her objections (Schwartz and DeKeseredy 1998). In a somewhat related argument, the same factors that
cause a man to abuse women may well also cause him to purchase
pornography. In other words, the woman abuse came first, followed by
his interest in pornography. In these scenarios, eliminating pornography
might not have an effect on the amount of woman abuse, since the men
are generally abusive anyway. However, this study and those that focused
on other groups of women demonstrate that pornography certainly is a
component of the problem of woman abuse (Bergen and Bogle 2000;
DeKeseredy and Schwartz 1998b; Funk 2006; Harmon and Check 1989;
Russell 1998).

Further, there is now evidence suggesting that rural boys consume
pornography more than do their urban counterparts, at least in the
Canadian province of Alberta. Also, many of these boys watch pornography with their male friends (see box 4.2). As Scott Bergthold, a U.S.
lawyer who helps small towns fight "adult business," told *Los Angeles
Times* reporter Stephanie Simon (2004, 2): "Rural communities never
thought they'd have to deal with what they perceived to be a big-city
problem." Obviously, things have changed, as "hard-core porn" has now
"hit the heartland." For example, the Lion's Den chain now has an "adult
superstore" in Quaker City, Ohio, population 563.

Other Characteristics of Men Who Sexually Assault Their Ex-Partners

Male partners' possession of firearms and their illegal drug use were
two other common themes respondents identified. For example, more
than half (58 percent) of the women said that male offenders had guns,
and some of them had threatened to use them.[7] Recall that Ashley's partner threatened to kill her with a shotgun if she left him (chapter 3);
another respondent told us that a man "busted" her eardrum with a
handgun.

Twenty-eight of the women (over 65 percent) said that their partners used illegal drugs and that their consumption of these substances
contributed to abusive behaviors.[8] One interviewee who desperately
wanted to leave her partner said:

4.2 ONE IN FOUR BOYS HEAVY PORN USERS, STUDY SHOWS

Boys aged 13 and 14 living in rural areas, are the most likely of their age group to access pornography, and parents need to be more aware of how to monitor their children's viewing habits, according to a new University of Alberta study.

A total of 429 students aged 13 and 14 from 17 urban and rural schools across Alberta, Canada, were surveyed anonymously about if, how and how often they accessed sexually explicit media content on digital or satellite television, video and DVD and the Internet. Ninety per cent of males and 70 per cent of females reported accessing sexually explicit media content at least once. More than one-third of the boys reported viewing pornographic DVDs or videos "too many times to count," compared to 8 per cent of the girls surveyed.

A majority of the students, 74 per cent, reported viewing pornography on the Internet. Forty-one per cent saw it on video or DVD and 57 per cent reported seeing it on a specialty TV channel. Nine per cent of the teens reported they accessed pornography because someone over 18 had rented it; 6 per cent had rented it themselves and 20 per cent viewed it at a friend's house.

The study also revealed different patterns of use between males and females, with boys doing the majority of deliberate viewing, and a significant minority planning social time around viewing porn with male friends. Girls reported more accidental or unwanted exposure online and tend to view porn in same-gender pairs or with mixed groups.

Though being curious about sexually explicit media may seem a 'natural' part of early adolescence, porn is a major presence in the lives of youth. The media environment in Alberta homes makes access to porn easy for teens and viewing pornography at a young age can set children up for problems later on, said Sonya Thompson, a master's graduate student at the University of Alberta in Edmonton, Canada, and author of the study. "We don't know how we are changing sexual behaviors, attitudes, values and beliefs by enabling this kind of exposure and not talking with kids about it in any meaningful way," Thompson said.

Thompson, formerly a sex education teacher, is concerned about the health and social messages pornography sends. Excessive early exposure to pornography may be harmful in terms of expectations going into relationships. "What kinds of expectations will these young people have going into their first sexual relationships? It may be setting up a big disconnect between boys and girls and may be normalizing risky sex practices."

Almost half of rural youths in the survey reported seeing pornographic videos or DVDs at least once, compared to one-third of the urban participants. Thompson is unsure why rural teens access porn more on video and DVD, but suggests that parents may think distance acts as a buffer. "Maybe they have a false sense of thinking they are far away from unhealthy influences." Rural boys also reported a lower incidence of parents talking with them about sexual media content. Urban girls were most likely to have had discussions with their parents.

And while the majority of teens surveyed said their parents expressed concern about sexual content, that concern hasn't led to discussion or supervision, and few parents are using available technology to block sexual content.

"It indicates there is plenty of room for better parenting around pornography use. Parents need to improve dialogue with their children and their own awareness level. They have to be educated enough to be the ones setting the boundaries in the house," Thompson said. "Families using media together is no longer the norm, so parents need to know what their kids have access to in their alone time," Thompson said.

Teachers also need to tackle the issue in sex education classes, she added. "Obviously it's a huge influence on kids and it needs to be talked about. There's a whole subculture we are not addressing."

Retailers, government and the media industry regulators also need to work with parents to ensure they are educated about limiting their children's access to sexually explicit material, have strategies to talk with their teens, and that laws around the sale of porn to minors are enforced, Thompson said.

Source: Betowski 2007, 1–2.

He quit drinking for a while and switched addictions and started doing cocaine. He started shooting cocaine with his insulin needles. He's also an insulin dependent diabetic, as well as a chronic alcoholic. He'd come home and force me to have sex with him, and it was like sleeping with a brewery. I would sit in the living room afterwards and he'd be passed out. And I'd think about how I could get away with killing him. I mean it was getting really bad. I just wanted, you know, I couldn't, like, escape him, you know.

Another woman told us a similar story. "Um, there were a lot of times that I had sex with him when I didn't want to," she said, "but there's one particular night that I do remember and it was towards the end of our relationship. It was a really bad relationship. We were always fighting. A lot of drugs involved. And he was really high and he kept coming at me, you know. . . . And then, of course, he would get together with his friends and do drugs and stuff. His drug of choice was heroin."

Some women told us that their partners' drug use was a key factor in motivating them to terminate their relationships.[9] Allison said, for example, that her ex-partner "was starting on coke right before we split up, because that was the whole drawing point for me was drugs. I was like, 'I'll deal with your drinking, 'cause you're the kid's dad, and, I mean, I didn't want the kids to not have a dad. His grandma says, 'Oh, he'll stop one of these days.' Which one?"

SUMMARY

Data presented in this chapter yield several conclusions. First, separation and divorce sexual assault occurs in some rural sections of Ohio, as it probably does in other parts of North America. Furthermore, like many survivors of wife rape and other forms of woman abuse, most of the women interviewed experienced multiple forms of victimization, including physical violence. This finding is consistent with studies that reveal the prevalence of "battering rapes" among women who are both physically and sexually assaulted by their male partners (Bergen 1996, 2006; Bergen and Bukovec 2006; Finkelhor and Yllo 1985; Russell 1990). Also, many participants were emotionally pressured to have sex against their will. This is not surprising, given that 79 percent of the women stated that the men who abused them strongly believed that they "should be in charge." As Bergen and Bukovec (2006) discovered: "Men who believe that they have a right, or entitlement to sex within their intimate relationships, often rely on emotional pressure or coercion to force their partners to comply."

Data presented in this chapter also provide further evidence that the sexual abuse of women is fostered by male peer support. Although the bulk of studies of this problem have been done on college campuses, this study supports what Lee Bowker (1983, 135–136) said more than twenty-five years ago about all-male patriarchal subcultures of violence:

> This is not a subculture that is confined to a single class, religion, occupational grouping, or race. It is spread throughout all parts of society. Men are socialized by other subculture members to accept common definitions of the situation, norms, values, and beliefs about male dominance and the necessity of keeping their wives in line. These violence-supporting social relations may occur at any time and in any place.

Another conclusion from the data presented here is that separation and divorce sexual assault is associated with men's consumption of pornography, possession of firearms, and use of alcohol and drugs. While many people would argue that the unknown number of men who consume pornography and never abuse women refutes the assertion that porn is a key determinant of sexual assault, as Russell (1998, 150) reminds us: "This is comparable to arguing that because some cigarette smokers don't die of lung disease, there cannot be a causal relationship between smoking and lung cancer. Only members of the tobacco industry and some seriously addicted smokers consider this a valid argument today." A large body of research shows that many women have been harmed or upset by their partners' requests or demands to imitate pornographic scenarios (Funk 2006).

That firearms, drugs, and alcohol were associated with many of the harms experienced by our respondents is to be expected, given that other studies found strong correlations between these factors and woman abuse (e.g., Campbell et al. 2003; Vigdor and Mercy 2006).

Consider, too, the results of a recent study that generated data from 8,529 men enrolled in Massachusetts certified batterer intervention programs between 1999 and 2003:

- Seven percent of the men reported owning guns during the past three years.
- Recent gun owners were 7.8 times more likely than non-gun owners to have threatened their partners with guns.
- Batterers reported using guns to threaten their partners in four ways, including threatening to shoot them, cleaning, holding or loading a gun during an argument, threatening to shoot a pet or person the victim cared about, and shooting a gun during an argument with a victim. (Rothman et al. 2005, 62)

Although he lacks conclusive evidence, Websdale contends that the abusive behaviors listed are probably more common in rural than in urban communities. He further argues that "rural culture, with its acceptance of firearms for hunting and self-protection, may include a code among certain men that accepts the casual use of firearms to intimidate wives and intimate partners. In urban areas it is more difficult for abusers to discharge their weapons and go undetected. People in the country are more familiar with the sound of gunshots and often attribute the sound to legitimate uses such as hunting" (1998, 10). Regardless of whether gun-related abuse is more common in rural than in urban settings, the women we interviewed revealed that drinking, drug use, and gun ownership is a "risky mix" (Sharps et al. 2003). Moreover, the consequences of experiencing the harms the women describe in this chapter are devastating.

CHAPTER 5

The Consequences of Abuse
and Women's Social Support
Experiences

> Jane . . . faces the ensuing police investigation and
> prosecution with little or no support from family and
> friends. She experiences a legal system that may place
> the blame for the incident on her, the victim. She lives
> in a community that does not want to believe "it"
> happens here—and if it does the woman must have
> asked for it. Jane is also facing the memory of
> childhood sexual abuse stirred up by this recent
> assault. Fortunately for her, however, there is a small
> rape crisis center that is able to provide her with
> support and advocacy. The center, which is under-
> funded, under-staffed and relies heavily on volunteers,
> will be there for Jane 24 hours a day as long as it takes.
> In essence Jane and the center will struggle together in
> the face of isolation and lack of resources.
>
> —Susan Lewis, *Unspoken Crimes*

JANE, THE WOMAN SUSAN LEWIS WRITES OF in the
chapter epigraph, did not participate in our study and is not a survivor
of separation or divorce sexual assault, and we do not know the rural area
where her husband's cousin raped her. But her experiences are similar to
those of many women we interviewed. A number of barriers indeed
exist to such rural women receiving social support services. As Logan et
al. (2004, 56) point out: "Rural areas have fewer available services and the
few that do exist must cover large geographic areas, the quality and con-
sistency of staff are problematic, and there are higher costs associated
with rural services while individuals in rural areas have fewer personal

resources to pay for costs."[1] This chapter describes, first, the consequences of the abuse of our forty-three women respondents, and, second, their social support experiences.

CONSEQUENCES OF ABUSE

Regardless of where it takes place, separation and divorce sexual assault, like other forms of woman abuse, changes the abused woman forever. Agnes told us, "It had a tremendous effect; it still has a tremendous effect." Patsy described some of the change she saw in herself: "I went through a big state of depression after all that. I was real depressed for quite a while. Um, I don't know, I just don't feel as whole anymore. I don't feel like I was as strong as I used to be before that, you know, I kind of feel weak. And, um, embarrassed."

Consistent with the findings of other studies, we found that the women we talked to had experienced a wide range of negative outcomes, including low self-esteem, fear, nightmares, and a myriad of physical health problems.[2] To be sure, the destructive consequences are immeasurable (Barnett et al. 2005). As reported by one interviewee: "Your health suffers. Your energy level is low. I'm miserable. I'm miserable and ashamed."

The women who participated in this study have experienced harms that few people are capable of imagining, and all of them are survivors. These strong and brave rural Ohio women have made great strides toward recovery, and all of them have plans for the future. In fact, one consistent response to our question about long-term goals is a plan to become actively involved in the struggle to end woman abuse. For example, Patricia said:

> I think that what I want to do is be a presenter in regards to domestic violence and sexual assault. I've worked with victims and just recently worked with perpetrators. I'm taking this summer off. Um, I'm taking an extended vacation and my plan is to get involved with um, educating, not only the community, but also education for the law enforcement, social workers, individuals who are counselors, the judicial system. I would love to be a part of developing policies. I think something that's, ah, advocacy. I would consider it to be like an indirect advocacy. That's my next—that's my plan, to move into that direction.

Other women, in addition to pursuing their career objectives, fully intend to fight back aggressively if they ever encounter a violent man. "I think it has taught me how to not ever let a man do something like this to you again," one interviewee told us. "And that is why I have butcher knives I sleep with. Stabbing is easy. And if someone comes into my bed again, I will kill them. I guarantee you they will be stabbed. I won't go to kill. You don't have to kill somebody. I don't have to cut his dick off. I don't have to do that stuff. I can cut his hand off."

Lori is another empowered survivor who will never take it again. "I mean, I'm doing way, way, way, way, way better now," she said. "And I could never imagine—I can't imagine being back in that position again, 'cause I have, I have such a low tolerance. If anyone pisses me off, I'm like, get out of my house right now or I'll call the police and get my bat! You know, I just have no tolerance. And I have no tolerance for anyone being controlling, violent, abusive toward women. I have no tolerance for it anymore."

Psychological Consequences

All the survivors we interviewed developed adverse postassault psychological conditions, such as depression, sexual aversion, and fear. This is what happened to Rita:

> I could care less if I ever have sex again in my life. I could care less if I ever had another relationship with a man again in my life. Oh, it's scarred me for life. I think it's physically, mentally—well, maybe not so much physically—but emotionally has scarred me for life. You know, and that's the reason why I don't socialize myself with people. I isolate myself from people because if I don't, I get panic attacks. And the dreams, they, they're never gone. They're never gone. I mean, I don't care how much you try to put it out of your head, the dreams always bring it back, always. I've been in a sleep clinic where they would videotape me sleeping, being in and out of bed, crawling into a corner screaming, "Please don't hurt me, don't shoot me, don't" whatever.

Other interviewees also frequently mentioned sexual aversion. Of this outcome, Carol told us: "Right now I'd have to say, sexually, I'm probably ruined. I don't ever want to have sex again with anyone. I have no desire to have sex with anyone." And another woman had similar feelings. "I really hate sex now. When somebody touches me, I just cringe, especially if there's alcohol on their breath. It's just a reminder of him crawling on top of me. So men that drink are the biggest turnoff ever, especially if they are wanting anything to do with sex and their drinking. It just, it turns my stomach! Still, [I] don't want in another relationship. I'm just scared they're all the same."

An intense mistrust of men in general was another common theme uncovered in our study. Laureen told us, for example:

> And years ago, years ago when I still only had one child, he told me he knew that I wanted out of the relationship and he said, "If I can't have you, I'm gonna make it so nobody can have you." And I didn't understand what he was talking about. And it was many, many years later that I realized he meant psychologically. He was going to destroy me psychologically so I wouldn't be fit to enter into another relationship. And it's basically true; I have not had any other relationship. I'm afraid to go into a relationship. I don't trust men in general. So basically I live a solitary life, not by choice, but because I'm afraid I'm going to end up in a relationship like that again.

Lori expresses similar mistrust: "I have a very low opinion of men in general. So that might have something to do with those experiences. I'm not really looking for any men. I've written them off. But I don't really associate with that many guys, period!"

We could offer many more examples of negative psychological outcomes. Often, the women experienced these psychological consequences in conjunction with physical injuries and the use of alcohol or drugs to dull both physical and psychological pains.

Physical Health Outcomes

We know that large numbers of women in ongoing heterosexual marital and cohabiting relationships experience both physical and sexual violence. We have found that this is also true when these women want to leave, are trying to leave, or have left their male partners. These sexual assaults have been termed by some scholars "battering rapes" (Bergen 1996, 2006; Finkelhor and Yllo 1985). Jackie, the target of such abuse, sustained severe physical injuries as a result. "He lowered my self-esteem," she told us of her ex-partner. "Um, I've got a lot of scars and I've still got four broken ribs over here, scars all over my face. I've got a knife stab wound here where he tried to stab me. I've got cuts around my private area, um, scars everywhere. Physically, he's, he's put damage on my body. Mentally as well 'cause I've got to get help to get over this, which I'm working on."

In addition to being raped and beaten and having her clothes torn up, another woman had to wait close to two weeks for the sheriff's department in her town to arrest her ex-partner:

> I'm kind of disappointed. I know this is not a good thing to say, but I'm disappointed in the sheriff's department because this happened to me on the tenth and Gary wasn't arrested for thirteen, you know, until thirteen days later. . . . They just kept dragging it out. They had a warrant and what not and I'm, like, four broken ribs. I'm laid out for two weeks on the couch. You know, eyes swollen shut, they had to have a warrant for his arrest and if they would have kicked him out that night I would still have a lot of things, you know, my car, you know, some of my, my clothes and shoes that he took. I mean right down to the underwear he took and tore up, all the things he tore up, I'd still have them.

Battering rapes are not restricted to intimate relationships, of course. A more distant family member raped Jane, the rural women mentioned in the epigraph of this chapter:

> The morning after a party hosted in her home by her abusive husband, Jane was given the task of driving the male guests home. After dropping one of them off, she was left in the car with her husband's cousin who offered to show her a shortcut to his house. Tired and wanting to get rid of him as quickly as possible, Jane agreed. The shortcut did not go to his house but rather to a strip-mining site far from anything else. The man forced Jane into the back seat of the car where he forcibly raped her. Afterward, he threw her out of the car and physically assaulted her. On instinct, Jane ran. Being in the middle of nowhere, she ran toward the sound of equipment running. She finally came upon a man driving heavy equipment,

approximately one mile from the site of her assault. The man called 911 in an effort to get some help for Jane. Because the site was in such a remote area, the police responding to the call got lost on their way. (Lewis 2003, 1)

Like Jackie, who suffered knife wounds and broken ribs, many of our respondents mentioned physical scars that bring back horrifying memories of events that could have led to their deaths. Jannie has physical scars all over her body from being thrown through a window. Lori, whose many scars stem from several brutal battering rapes committed by her estranged male partner, told us: "I have dents in my legs where he used to kick me, and some scarring, you know, in different places."

Some women, such as one we interviewed from a small Ohio town, suffered from other health problems related to ongoing sexual assaults. "I haven't had an orgasm in years," she told us. "My girl parts are extremely painful. It's hard to wash down there because I've had so many urinary tract infections. I think it's a form of having sex so rough and so vigorous so many times that, um, it's very sensitive to those things."

To cope with these and other physical consequences, some women we interviewed turned to drugs or alcohol. Lorraine ended up an alcoholic.[3] "I am a recovering alcoholic," she told us. "I would get really drunk and pass out, and I would have these nightmares of my past stepfathers molesting me, and you know. I would throw things in my vagina and in my dreams I would be running and running and I couldn't get away from it. Like I would wake up, and it would be him and that really messes with me in any way possible."

Other women in the process of leaving knew that sexual assaults were imminent and took drugs to prevent their partners from sexually assaulting them. Judy, one of several respondents who used this strategy, said, "I, um, found myself taking my pain pills more often just so I wouldn't have to be awake when he came home."

Unfortunately, criminal justice officials and other support providers stigmatize or look down on many women who drink or take drugs to dull the pain of abuse. This was the case for the interviewee who told us: "I didn't have any resources after he beat me up very badly. I went to the police and filed a report, and due to the fact that they knew me from some of my drinking episodes, they treated me with a lot of disrespect." As Colleen Ward (1995, 76) reminds us: "On the whole, women are expected to play traditional gender roles and to restrict their behaviors accordingly. There is little sympathy for women who are judged to be daring, careless or imprudent."

Respondents whose partners were sexually active with other women ran the risk of acquiring a sexually transmitted disease (STD), as Joan acknowledged: "I have a fear of, you know, of like, having some type of disease or something like that." Indeed, some women are so scared of getting an STD that they go to clinics for frequent HIV tests. However, it is unclear whether any women we interviewed actually became infected.

Financial Outcomes

The respondents' mean income for 2002 was $13,588. Such a low income makes it extremely difficult for women to leave abusive men or those they no longer love. At the time this study was conducted, abused women and others needing social support from government agencies faced major obstacles, as they still do today. For example, the local Department of Jobs and Family Services budget was cut by $9 million in 2001 (Evans 2002). During the same time, a local battered women's shelter received $17,801 less in funding, and the crisis hotline in the same city was "scaled back considerably" due to rising statewide Medicaid costs and requirements for local agencies to match Medicaid funding (Claussen 2003).

Finding a quality job in the current political and economic climate is a major challenge, especially for rural women lacking formal education. The closing of sawmills, coalmines, and other key sources of jobs has economically devastated many rural towns in the area that had relied them for employment (DeKeseredy, Donnermeyer et al. 2007; L. Jensen 2006).[4] Other broader social and economic structural changes, such as farm closings, have transformed entire rural communities and today account for the persistently high levels of unemployment and poverty many of them confront (K. Johnson 2006; Lobao and Meyer 2001). As Gallup-Black (2005, 165) observed when considering the vast literature on the strong linkage between disadvantage and homicide in urban locations: "The relationship between violence and economic hardship . . . defined by job loss, unemployment, poverty, and population loss—can be just as pronounced in rural or small population areas."

Mary summed it up for many women who exit a relationship: "Economically? I'm at the bottom of the food chain now." These women endured not only physical, psychological, and sexual abuse from their partners before and after leaving them, but also, in 70 percent of the cases, economic abuse. There are many examples of negative financial outcomes for the women we interviewed, including difficulties finding housing and inability to get proper nutrition and clothes for their children. However, many financial difficulties were often related to inadequate social support services and an absence of collective efficacy in the women's communities.

PERCEPTIONS OF COLLECTIVE EFFICACY AND SAFETY

Many people contend that our respondents' experiences are unique among rural women, because, they claim, rural areas have higher levels of collective efficacy than do urban ones. In a broad-ranging semi-structured interview schedule covering a number of factors that we felt might be related to separation and divorce sexual assault, it was impossible to use all the questions Sampson, Raudenbush, and Earls (1997) developed to measure collective efficacy in urban neighborhoods. We did ask our respondents these modified versions of items that study included, which measure informal social control and social cohesion and trust: (1) How often do you get together with your neighbors in a typical week? (2) Could you count on your neighbors to help you solve your personal problems?

To acquire more information about the women's perceptions of their communities, we also asked if they personally know other women who have been raped or sexually assaulted; if they thought that unwanted sex, rape, and sexual assault are major problems in their communities; how safe they felt when they were at home; and what type of help they asked for and/or received.

Unfortunately for our respondents, their communities were hardly supportive. Rather, it is not unfair to say that the communities functioned in ways that promoted a great deal of pain and suffering. For example, most interviewees (84 percent) stated that women's experiencing unwanted sex in their community is a major problem and 81 percent reported that rape or sexual assault is also a serious problem.

Macy is one of many respondents who perceived sexual assault as "being rampant" in her town:

> It's a big problem. And, a lot of people get by with it. A lot of people! Even these fifteen- year-old kids that are touching these seven-year-old kids are getting by with it. Yeah, and everything is getting way out of hand. Nobody is doing nothing but slapping everybody on the hands and it's justified. And it's not justified, what you take from that child or woman or man is not justified, because . . . when you go and take from them, that is something you took that will never be given back from nobody. Nobody can refill something that has been taken from you.

Some people might argue that such perceptions are heavily influenced by a woman's own victimization. However, that 81 percent of the respondents stated that they personally know other women who were sexually assaulted provides further evidence that such victimization is a major problem in some rural areas and that little is being done to prevent it. Jayne knows more than one woman in her community who has either been raped or sexually assaulted in other ways. "With the girls I know," she said, "all of them have had at least one sexual assault experience, if not rape, and mostly it goes unreported because they feel that they're at fault or it's an isolated situation that this person wouldn't do it otherwise."

Some women graphically described what happened to their friends, neighbors, or relatives, as did this interviewee: "I have a girlfriend. She's been married for twenty-one years . . . and her husband uses anything, like screwdrivers and, and anything he can get a hold of to shove up her. And the Bible says you're supposed to submit to your husband. And in her mind submitting means let him do whatever he wants."

A number of sexual assaults known to our respondents were committed not only by current or former husbands, common-law partners, and boyfriends, but also by uncles, brothers, or fathers. "I know a lot of people that were molested, including myself," an interviewee told us, "by their father, by their uncle, by their brother, you know. And, at first, in your head you think that's the way you are supposed to interact. It's because it was a normal thing, and then you start to realize over time you just let these men treat you worse and worse and worse. And you just get to this point like, wow, where is my self-respect?"

Given their own experiences of separation and divorce sexual assault and their knowledge of others who have had similar experiences, it is not surprising that more than half (58 percent) of the interviewees do not feel safe at home, especially since forced sex is strongly related to homicide (Campbell et al. 2003). Sometimes, too, "children can become unfortunate pawns in the violent games" played by male ex-partners (Polk 1994, 43), which is one of the key reasons many interviewees' children also feel unsafe at home. Agnes's son, for example, has a well-founded fear of being killed based on the abuse he and his mother endured during the process of her leaving her husband. "My son automatically locks the doors when he gets into the house," Agnes told us. "He only sleeps with the dog. He has to have the dog in his room at night because that's his warning signal."

As suggested earlier, that the men who abuse these women have strong social ties with male peers who also sexually or physically assault women exacerbates the fear of many of these women. Twenty of them (47 percent) stated that their estranged partners' friends engaged in these types of woman abuse, and that some perpetrators enlisted the help of their friends to sexually assault some of the interviewees. Moreover, pro-abuse male peer support sometimes occurs in settings intended to stop men from being abusive:

> He had to go to domestic violence counseling every Monday for six months, but sending him to that counseling meant that I got beat every Monday night for six months. Because he would come home madder than hell because he had to go to that place. It was just the most horrible thing I could ever done to him and it wasn't me. I told the judge, "I don't care what you do to him, but don't send him to counseling." And she sent him back there anyway. So every Monday for six more months I got beaten because he had to go for three hours and sit in class. . . . And then we meet up with a few of the guys from his class and I think they all did it. Because they were all mad every Monday night and a few of the women I talked to, they're

like, "Yep, they come in extra mad because it's your fault we have to be there." I was like, For what? I don't hit you. So it was just the worst help ever.

NONINTERVENTION NORMS
AND CUTTING OFF CONTACT

A growing literature shows that neighbors are more likely to help each other out in urban communities with high levels of collective efficacy than in those with low levels (Sampson, Raudenbush, and Earls 1997; Taylor 2001). However, most of our rural respondents felt that their friends and neighbors adhered to and enforced "nonintervention norms" (Browning 2002). For example, 84 percent of the women stated that they could not count on their neighbors to help solve their personal problems. This woman's response is a case in point: "You know, my neighbors, I mean they could hear it, they could see it, they could hear the glass, they could see me being locked out of the house in underwear and just cut up from one end to the other. . . . So I didn't get any help from anybody. I had to do it all on my own."

In some cases, neighbors did not help because the women were too embarrassed to reveal their pain and suffering to "the folks next door" or because privacy norms dictated that they "keep their mouths shut," which is also a key barrier to obtaining formal support services in rural communities (Logan et al. 2004). As June pointed out when asked about her ties with neighbors: "Back then you never really talked about things like that with other women. So I really don't know. I didn't share. I kept everything a secret. I didn't want anybody to know what was going on. You know, you try to keep everything painted pretty and, you know, we lived in a subdivision, where the only thing that separated your house was a driveway. So, uh, you didn't talk a lot about your personal affairs to your neighbors."

Recall that 79 percent of the sample said that their partners strongly believed that men should be in charge of the household, which partly also explains why 67 percent of the sample did not get together with their neighbors in a typical week and thus could not count on them for help. Her partner's being in charge often restricted a woman's day-to-day activities, "cutting [her] off from the outside world." For example, even if her neighbors had been willing to help her, Pat could not report her abusive experiences to them because she "was only allowed to be around people at work basically." Jackie's ex-partner laid down similar rules because "he thought that he was all I needed. You know, a measure of love was that I could get all my needs met from him."

Men's fear of facing negative sanctions for their abusive conduct was another factor that contributed to their cutting their partners off from contact with neighbors. For example, Mandy said, "I had black and blue marks on me, so you know he didn't want somebody to see that." A few women said that their neighbors did not help them because they were experiencing similar problems. June said that "a lot" of her neighbors were in relationships characterized by frequent marital rape, wife beating, and other forms of male-to-female victimization. Her male neighbors condoned and engaged in woman abuse, while their partners were involved in an ongoing struggle to maintain their own safety and did not have the time or energy to help others.

In sum, in addition to facing barriers to formal means of social support (see Logan et al. 2005; Logan et al. 2004), many rural survivors of separation and divorce sexual assault cannot rely on informal processes of social control. This is not to say, however, that the women we interviewed suffered in total silence. For example, 58 percent turned to at least one friend for help, but most of their friends did not live near them. Further, 44 percent sought assistance from the police, and 40 percent received help from a local shelter.

SOCIAL SUPPORT EXPERIENCES

The interviewees revealed that in the short term, formal and better intervention by state authorities is a more important focus for them than is collective efficacy. Perhaps this is because, as several studies have found, many rural legal officials and other service providers contribute to a collective efficacy that protects or encourages woman abuse.[5] Among Marlene's recommendations:

> And then with the criminal justice system, start doing something from the beginning. You know, stop this shit. Just because he was a correctional officer with this political stuff, you know, they don't want his name in the newspaper or whatever, you know. I don't

know whether that goes from the get-go, you know, on how we choose our police officers, you know, and so on and so forth. I mean, I know that there's um, you're going to have these kinds of people wherever you go, but this was a whole community, you know.

Cultures, whether they are urban or rural, "live through word of mouth and example" (Jacobs 2004, 5). Most respondents perceive their communities' cultures as patriarchal and view an unknown number of formal service providers as setting "a bad example" for others. Again, on top of paying selective attention to the voices of survivors, many rural agents of social control are part of a good ol' boy network that includes members who degrade and abuse women (Websdale 1998). For example, based on her brutal experiences, Jolene contends:

> Cops are number-one bad for unwanted sex, for forcing unwanted sex on their mates and violence. They've got to change the whole structure of the protective system with more women on the force. They're all men—how's a man gonna relate to what a woman just went through? It's a good ol' boys network. And it's terrible that our police have come to that. They're not protection.

Who knows more about abuse than those who suffer from it? Unfortunately, many lawmakers do not view survivors as leading experts on intimate violence, and they often develop policies such as mandatory prosecution that are not supportive of abused women's interests or needs (Ford 2003). As Bergen (1996) discovered, police officers, spiritual and religious advisors, advocates for battered women, and quite a variety of other social support resources do not provide sufficient support to victims of wife rape. Data derived from her survey of 1,730 service providers across the United States reveal that only 33.5 percent of the women's agencies included in her sample taught their staff and volunteers about marital rape survivors' legal rights, resources available to them, and their emotional reactions to sexual abuse, and about ways of identifying marital rape survivors. If women raped by their live-in partners do not receive proper assistance, it is logical to assume that survivors of separation and divorce sexual assault get even less social support.

The women we interviewed had a low opinion of criminal justice agencies. Of the women who turned to at least one element of that system for help, only one stated that it was the best assistance she had received. In sharp contrast to her experience, a woman who resided in the same rural community said, "The police department was worthless." In another town, the justice of the peace discouraged a respondent from filing a restraining order "on the grounds," Maggie reported, "that ah, it was only a piece of paper." Elements of the criminal justice system (e.g., courts and police), in fact, were ranked as the worst form of social support by twelve (28 percent) of the interviewees.

Most interviewees, however, turned to several different sources of social support, including friends (58.14 percent) and local shelters (39.53 percent). The bulk of the women we spoke with viewed friends as the best source of social support. This is not surprising; other woman abuse studies that used methods like ours also found friends rated highly (e.g., Bowker 1983). Family members and shelters ranked second, followed by mental health workers.

Only a few women mentioned spiritual leaders, religious communities, or places of worship during the course of our conversations with them. Nevertheless, what some of them told us strongly suggested, as one interviewee put it, that it "was pointless turning to them for help." In the view of this woman's congregation, what happened to her

> wasn't outright rape, you know, like a stranger coming into your house on a dark night or something like that. I was married to the person and it didn't look like I was wanting to refuse. . . . You have to set a good example of a Christian submissive wife. Submission is very big to Jehovah's Witnesses. And if I went against the elders, then it went against me in the congregation. So—and they didn't think women had brains to begin with—so I had no support. . . . My people, my social support, was telling me to go right back into it. There wasn't anybody else.

Another respondent recalled a similar experience after she publicly revealed her abuse. "The community kind of turns against you when you do this," she recalled. "See, I was living in a Catholic neighborhood and they don't care what it is, you stay with that man. So I was kind of judged a lot in the community."

One woman did find help in her religious community. "I guess my best support came through finding God and my church family when I moved here," she told us. "Because my mom and the rest of my family, they were like five hours away and they provided the space for me, but my church family has been my biggest refuge thus far."

In identifying the worst help they received, eleven women said "no one." They answered this way because they had next to no contact with anyone who could help them. Hence, they could not make what they defined as valid comparisons. Regardless of the quality of their experiences, however, every respondent needed help to cope with abuse and actively sought social support. Still, not one respondent mentioned going to a hospital or a general practitioner, which is likely the result of lacking health insurance, facing other cost barriers, or having problems getting appointments with medical personnel (Logan et al. 2004).[6] (There may be social services these women were not aware of, a topic taken up in chapter 6.)

Summary

The harms uncovered by our study generated major negative outcomes, and researchers and theorists need to rethink the concept of collective efficacy. Again, what is perceived as for the common good often may include behaviors and discourses that threaten the health and wellbeing of women seeking freedom from patriarchal oppression. Although the respondents perceived an absence of effective informal social control, their own policy recommendations focused primarily on improvement in three areas: formal support services, education, and public awareness (see chapter 6).

Most of the women who turned to elements of the criminal justice system for assistance did not hold them in high regard. While perceptions such as theirs are hardly exclusive to rural locations (Hogg and Carrington 2006), some of the data presented in this chapter strongly suggest that major improvements to the criminal justice system's response to separation and divorce sexual assault in rural communities need to be made. That fewer service options are available to survivors in rural areas, as stated earlier, also partly explains why some respondents had no contact with anyone who could help them. Still, of all the social support resources identified by the interviewees, friends came out on top.

Chapter 6

Where Do We Go from Here?

Research, Theory, and Policy

> While stranger-on-stranger violence is much less
> frequent in rural areas, violence among intimates is as
> frequent in rural areas as in cities. However, there is
> too little research to say much more with any
> confidence. There are many unanswered questions
> about rural domestic violence, including both spouse
> abuse and child abuse.
>
> —Ralph A. Weisheit, David N. Falcone,
> and L. Edward Wells, *Rural Crime and Rural Policing*

Data presented throughout this book and gathered by a small number of urban wife rape studies show that exiting or trying to exit a marital or cohabiting relationship increases women's chances of being sexually assaulted, especially if the women are connected to patriarchal or abusive men. However, there is still much that we do not know about the problem of separation and divorce sexual assault in rural and urban communities. Obviously, much more empirical and theoretical work is needed. It is also necessary to develop policies and practices that meet the unique needs of women who are terrorized by the men who will not let them leave and men whom they have left. This chapter provides suggestions for future research and theorizing and also suggests policies based on the needs and voices of rural survivors.

New Directions in Empirical Work

Whether separation and divorce sexual assault studies are conducted in rural or urban settings, we need data from men to more precisely determine what motivates them to be abusive (DeKeseredy, Rogness, and

Schwartz 2004; Jewkes et al. 2006). Certainly, we obtain a great deal of useful information by asking the people who know these men best—the women who share or have shared their lives, who can speak extensively, for example, on men's behavior or the correlates of men's behavior (such as the influence of male peers or alcohol). Still, such information does not obviate the need for direct research on men. As Diana Scully points out (1990, 4), there are problems in depending completely on female partners to report on male sexual abusers, because "they do not share the reality of sexually violent men. Such insight is acquired through invading and critically examining the social constructions of men who rape."

This is not to say that we cannot learn much about the risk factors associated with separation and divorce sexual assault by asking women questions about the men who harmed them. For example, our study identified key determinants of such assault such as male peer support and patriarchal control.

In their research on crime in rural Australia and the societal reactions to it, Hogg and Carrington (2006, 79) found that violence against women is strongly associated with a rural hegemonic masculinity that "subordinates others through practices of domination that historically have relied on the exercise of violence." Is this the case in various rural areas in the United States? Further, do threats to rural hegemonic masculine identity such as those discovered by Hogg and Carrington in rural Australia contribute to rural separation and divorce sexual assault in the United States? Examples of these threats are the growth of rural women's movements, tougher drinking and driving laws, and the crisis in family farming. These empirical questions can be answered only empirically and more in-depth research on men would definitely address this concern.

Representative sample surveys of rural and urban populations help determine the incidence and prevalence of separation and divorce sexual assault. Such rural research is difficult to do because of the methodological obstacles discussed in chapter 3. Further, many other groups of men and women need to be included in future research, such as those who are immigrants, live in public housing, have physical disabilities, and so on. Some members of these groups were included in this study, but it is difficult to know whether the population was adequately represented among the women.

Following Christopher Browning (2002), this is one of the first studies to apply collective efficacy theory to woman abuse in intimate heterosexual relationships. However, this project is distinct from his and others like it (e.g., DeKeseredy, Alvi et al. 2003) because it examines the link between community characteristics and separation and divorce sexual assault in rural communities. Additional research is needed in this arena, including studying the perceptions and experiences of rural women who are not abused. Another point to consider is that almost all studies of collective efficacy/social disorganization and crime use quantitative techniques, such as analyses of census data. Many rural social problems are not easy to study using such methods, which is perhaps one of the key reasons why so few researchers focus on woman abuse in rural areas (Websdale 1998).

Further, quantitative methods alone cannot adequately describe the complexities of rural woman abuse and community responses to it (DeKeseredy and Schwartz 2008). Thus, it is essential to continue "going beyond census data" to examine community characteristics that affect separation and divorce sexual assault and other forms of woman abuse (Osgood and Chambers 2000). One suggestion is specifically to design a qualitative project that focuses exclusively on the topics of central concern to this book and that uses in-depth interviews and participant observations of community relations. Websdale's (1998) research is an outstanding example of such a study. He rode with police officers, observed woman abuse cases in court, talked to battered women, interviewed agents of social control, and actually lived in eastern Kentucky, the region of his study. Similarly, Hogg and Carrington's (2006) rural Australian study serves as an excellent model for developing a study of community characteristics related to various forms of woman abuse.[1]

Other directions for future research include the continued use of broad definitions of sexual assault, the use of multiple measures of sexual assault (DeKeseredy 1995; Mahoney and Williams 1998; Smith 1994), and studies of abuse that occurs when women try to terminate or have terminated relationships with boyfriends that do not live with them. Regardless of the methods or topics selected for research, it is important to develop and test theories of separation and divorce sexual assault. Certainly, "the purpose of all theory is to understand and explain" (Einstadter and Henry 1995, 12), and in addition to serving as conceptual tools that help us make sense of data, theories are practical. For example, to cure AIDS, researchers must first identify the cause of this deadly disease. In fact, almost every policy developed to prevent or control crimes like those committed against the women who participated in this study originated in a theory or theories (DeKeseredy, Ellis, and Alvi 2005).

NEW DIRECTIONS IN THEORETICAL WORK

The theoretical model offered in chapter 2 (supported by results presented in chapter 4) serves as a starting point for future theoretical work, and subsequent offerings need to address some "rural realities" conspicuously lacking there (see figure 2.1).[2] For example, most theories of woman abuse developed and evaluated thus far focus primarily on female victimization in urban communities. Heavily informed by data uncovered by this study; by theories developed by DeKeseredy and Schwartz (2002) and DeKeseredy, Rogness, and Schwartz (2004); and by research done by Hogg and Carrington in six rural Australian communities, we address this gap in the theoretical literature by offering a rural masculinity crisis / male peer support theory of separation and divorce sexual assault (see figure 6.1).

Developed by DeKeseredy, Donnermeyer et al. (2007), rural social and economic transformations and the role of male peer support are major components of this theory. Following Scott Sernau (2006, 69), their model asserts that in rural communities, "male privilege is persistent but precarious." For example, until the end of the twentieth century, many rural men obtained an income from either owning family farms or working in extractive industries such as coal mining (L. Jensen 2006; Lobao and Meyer 2001; Sherman 2005). Buttressed by patriarchal ideology, these men's marriages were typically characterized by a rigid gendered division of labor in which men were the primary breadwinners and women had "an intense and highly privatized relationship with domestic production,"

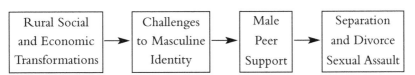

6.1. A Rural Masculinity Crisis / Male Peer Support Model
of Separation and Divorce Sexual Assault

such as rearing children and doing housework (Websdale 1998, 49; Fassinger and Schwarzweller 1984). Although such gender relations are still evident in a sizeable number of rural communities, rural men's power has become fragile as rural social and economic transitions over the last forty or more years have presented major challenges to their masculine identity (Campbell and Bell 2000; Jobes 1997; Sherman 2005).

For example, there has been a major decline in the number of family-owned farms because many people cannot make a reasonable living from them (Jacobs 2004). Moreover, as stated in chapter 5, the closing of sawmills, coalmines, and other key sources of income have devastated economically many rural U.S. communities that relied on a small number of industries for employment (L. Jensen 2006). Many women seek employment or get jobs when their husbands become unemployed or when their farms become less profitable—another factor that has the potential for weakening the overall power of men (Albrecht, Albrecht, and Albrecht 2000; Lasley et al. 1995; Lobao and Meyer 2001). This transition in the arena of employment often generates marital instability, because many economically displaced males who cannot meet their perceived responsibilities as the man of the household feel deprived of intimate and social support resources that give them self-worth (Harris and Bologh 1985). A sizeable portion of unemployed rural men who strongly adhere to the ideology of familial patriarchy compensate for their lack of economic power by exerting more control over their wives (DeKeseredy, Ellis, and Alvi 2005; Sherman 2005), a problem that can influence these women to consider leaving or to exit their marriages. Numerous other major social and economic transitions have spawned "the crisis in the rural gender order" (Hogg and Carrington 2006, 181), such as women's rights to own property and inherit wealth, an increase in the number of rural women's associations, and the "delegitimation" of some forms of rural masculinity (e.g., via tougher drinking and driving laws).

Some unemployed rural men have "managed to remake masculinity" in ways that do not involve intense patriarchal domination and control of their wives (Sherman 2005, 31). For example, Sherman's (2005) study of families harmed by the closure of sawmills in a rural California community reveals that some unemployed men became active fathers and enjoyed spending much time with their children while their wives worked. Other unemployed rural men, however, deal with the masculinity challenges by spending a great deal of time drinking with men in similar situations, and this is one of the key reasons why their wives leave or try to leave them. Further, as suggested by some data presented in chapter 4, many rural men have peers who view wife beating, rape, and other forms of male-to-female victimization as legitimate and effective means of repairing "damaged patriarchal masculinity" (Messerschmidt 1993; Raphael 2001). Similar to many of their unemployed urban counterparts, these men serve as abusive role models (see chapter 2).

When women terminate relationships because of their partners' substance abuse, violent behavior, or other problems generated in part by unemployment, rural men often perceive this move as yet another threat to their masculinity. We believe (in line with the theory described in chapter 2 and with figure 6.1) that male peers influence some rural men to engage in separation and divorce sexual assault to regain control and to avoid losing status among their friends. Patriarchal domination and control, frequent drinking with friends, and other variants of male peer support are related to the abuse uncovered by our study. Moreover, like explanations of other rural crimes, the model briefly discussed here addresses the fact that rural women's individual abusive experiences are parts "of a larger set of economic and social structural factors" (Donnermeyer, Jobes, and Barclay 2006, 201).

Regardless of which current or new theory best explains the causes of the pain and suffering described throughout this book, for women like those who participated in this study, the creation of effective public and legal policies should be the top priority. And, as Logan et al. (2004, 58) correctly point out, "creative solutions must be developed in order to serve women with victimization histories within the context of the specific communities where these women live."

Women's Policy Recommendations

Our respondents' statements about inadequate sources of support are consistent with those made by women who participated in other rural woman abuse studies (e.g., Logan et al. 2004). While urban women encounter many barriers to service, rural women by comparison have fewer resources, and those that are available cover very large geographic areas. "There's not a lot of jobs here," one woman told us. "Without a car I'm kind of dead. It's really hard without a car. So, um, there has to be,

I don't think there's any help in the county for someone in my situation. And without help, I don't know how I'm going to be able to get out of the county. . . . I have actual plans, but I don't know how they are ever going to come to fruition because I'm stuck economically. And right now my health is just a tad not good."

Another woman was caught in a similar trap, and so was her girlfriend, and the odds are against their escaping it:

Um, yeah, I mean I do go to counseling and I still was going to counseling throughout the, like I told you, almost the last fifteen years, but there's only so much a counselor can do for you. There's no places women can go if they are in need, really. You have to drive quite a bit a ways away from this area to get anywhere, or if you're controlled by your other person you can't drive, can't go anywhere unless you get permission or you can't take the vehicle, you're screwed. You can't get help. I mean, the closest shelter in this area, as far as I know, is Defiance, and I don't even know if they're still open 'cause they got a lot of budget cuts, so there ain't nothing for nobody anymore. And I mean, like, my girlfriend down the road, she's been wanting to leave her husband for years, since her daughter was seven years old she's been wanting to leave her husband, but she can't because she can't do it on her own. And he, you know, there ain't nothing, I mean. I ain't financially, I mean this time, I wanted to leave Stan and they didn't even, they couldn't even help me at all to find a place. The Victims of Crime got their budget cut, and the only way they could help me is if I left him for definite, but see if I left him for definite I couldn't have no transportation, I wouldn't have no money coming in. And, and if I would have moved, all they would have done was pay my deposit. Well, how am I gonna pay rent if I'm not working? You understand what I mean?

Here we offer survivors' perspectives on effective means of social support and intervention. Certainly, we can learn much from listening to them.

Educating

As Mary said, "My big push is always education," and education on the issue of woman abuse is one of the most common suggestions our forty-three respondents provided. Another woman makes the case clearly:

Education, education, education. Because you know what? I think that the first step in prevention, any type of prevention, is educating both genders, all races, all religions, everything. If you educate and explain to a population that this behavior is unwanted because it hurts another human being. Not because it is wrong or morally wrong, but because it is inhumane. And so because of that, well, I think that is a good enough reason for education and say, "Hey, look, this is inhuman behavior. This is unacceptable, period!"

Others had similar views, including Jane, who said we need to get on with

educating men and women about their rights and uh, that sex is not an entitlement in a relationship or in anything. And that, ya know, men need to be taught from boys that—and I mean its contradictory to the whole of society so it's really, I mean, how can you say it's, ya know, you're two years old [and] from the time you're anywhere you're seeing naked women and like the whole imagery, like, encourages it, excuses any kind of victimization, like "Boys will be boys" kind of bullshit. So, I think men need to take responsibility for the fact that there is something really wrong. Just with trying to control someone just because, I don't know, you have low self-esteem or whatever the hell your damn problem is. And women need to know that they don't have to, they need to be taught that they don't have to be submissive. And that's not what they're taught, basically. They're taught to do the exact opposite. So education, I think. . . . Um, well, I think that the only way to really—it's just such a huge thing to the whole basis of the capitalist system. I mean, you're selling sex and so because it sells the best.

CREATING AWARENESS. Creating awareness that a problem exists is part of an effective education process, and like the rural sexual assault advocates interviewed by Lewis (2003), many of our respondents believed that this would be a useful step. "I think awareness," Louise said. "I think girls growing up in this community don't get a lot of awareness about domestic violence. It's touched on briefly. They don't realize the warning signs of it and they need to get out. Because it won't get any better. It's not going to change no matter how much you love him, it won't change."

Robby's suggestions took a similar tack: "Education, ya. Public aware-ness, public awareness—because it's such a touchy subject. I don't know, kind of almost like a taboo. You know, it's like, and it's, it's, just, ya, we need to talk about it. Need to talk about it. Get it out there. Let people know that there is help, you know, because if there is a woman who is experiencing that and they see that I know, . . . maybe that will help women step out and get some help."

PROVIDING INFORMATION. Another facet of educating the public is providing accurate information. The women just quoted are concerned with teaching women and men that sexual assaults on women are unac-ceptable behaviors; the follow-up is information about where women can go for help once it happens to them. Many women we talked to did not know of a single existing service to which they could turn. If these services do exist in a local community, then Debbie's suggestion needs to be taken seriously, and that is

> getting some information out. I don't know if, ah, I don't know if maybe your public health services, ah, I don't know if they had posters or anything like that, that would advertise their services. Because I know that, you know, quite a few people go to the health department or something like that for medical health. And if they're having problems with the type of situation, maybe a poster or some-thing with information on that particular topic could trigger something inside of that woman, that particular woman. Then maybe she would reach out, you know, talk to somebody.

Of course, it is a longer road to solving the problem of separation and divorce sexual assault than just providing information. Joan is well aware that much more than pamphlets are necessary, but she retains a strong belief that they can help in raising awareness:

> Um, I think that awareness, somehow get awareness out there through human services, um, you know, the welfare department, so on and so forth. You can get pamphlets out that women don't have to put up with it. You know, um, like I said, the first place for it to start is with awareness, you know, in, in the community like within the welfare office, maybe WIC office, whatever offices that especially

young women or women that are, um, not educated, you know. And even if you are educated, it doesn't make any difference. I was educated. I went to school for human services. I went to school for all that. I mean, victim abuse and victim counseling. I mean, I went to school to counsel people and it was happening to me. So, even women that are educated it can happen to. But, if you can, you know, if they can be more aware, if the women can be more aware then maybe it would at least take the numbers down.

Training Local Practitioners

Next to educating the public, an equally important recommendation from a survivor is to train shelter workers and other practitioners to recognize separation and divorce sexual assault and to deliver services that directly match survivors' needs.

"There's a big difference between domestic violence and sexual abuse," Sue points out. "It's just not there. I mean, you could call the Crisis Center, you know, and they're like, they're dumbfounded. You know, 'cause they're not used to that kind of crisis call coming in. It just needs to be out there and somebody needs to be trained to take these calls. It's just like at the shelter. They don't understand, you know, they don't live, they're not trained to deal with it."

Listening to the Voices of Survivors

Before effective steps can be taken to alleviate separation and divorce sexual assault in rural and other communities, our society must first recognize that it exists. As we have seen, too many women suffer in silence, and when they do cry for help, rarely do members of their communities respond. As one survivor told us, "People have to be, you know, listen, and um, be sympathetic in relation to what exactly happened." Many other interviewees emphasized the importance of listening to survivors' voices and developing sensitivity to women's needs and pain. Jane's advice was direct: people need to "listen. Listen to what they [the women] have to say. Don't jump to conclusions and tell them that they're liars or it will be okay, to get over it." Jackie made a similar suggestion:

Listen to the victim. Understand how traumatic that experience may have been. Also what needs to be understood is how that experience is going to affect that person in the future and any children that may be in that home. My twelve-year-old for the last three years—well, since we have split up—has put the couch in front of the door and that's where he sleeps every single night. Because he's only twelve and he's a big kid, but he's not that big. He said that way, if he can stop him in any way until I can get to a phone or get out of the house, he'll do it.

For the woman we quoted earlier who had difficulties with the Jehovah's Witness community in her town, listening and believing should go hand in hand. First, she suggests, respect the women enough to

> believe them. I wasn't believed. When I said yes, there's drugs, yes, there's guns, yes, there's been violence, there's abuse, there's a history of abuse, he's threatened to abuse my daughters, he's beating my children, I wasn't believed. Even when I am sitting in the police station and the person, my son, is admitting it and also my husband admitted freely to the Jehovah's Witness elders the abuses and the drugs and the every kind of tax evasion, different things he did. You know, he would admit it to them, but not to the justice system. He got caught a couple of times and had to go to court for things he did. I wasn't believed. He was always believed. How can that be?

Rita said one of the hardest things is simply getting listeners to "believe what it is you're telling them. Sometimes you'll tell somebody what exactly happened, it's like, oh no, it didn't happen that way. But that is the way it happened. Why would you make up something like that? I mean, trying to come up with a story like that, it's not, it wouldn't be easy."

Reforming Elements of the Criminal Justice System

Most interviewees were dissatisfied with the criminal justice system's response to their victimization. They had many suggestions for improvement, a number of which centered on more punitive means of dealing with abusers. "I think they need to be . . . more strict on the perpetrator," Loreen said. Pat wanted tougher laws against stalkers:

> Stalking, stalking is horrible and um, there should be stronger laws about that. My understanding is there isn't anything they can do

about that until after something bad happens, and so with domestic violence they have to wait until she gets hit first. So it seems to me that there should be some protection for women if they feel unsafe or feel threatened and not actually have to come limping in, you know. So if whatever system it comes under, if its law enforcement or whatever, uh, more money needs to be spent on shelters and more money needs to be spent on prosecuting abusers. It's too bad it's hard to prove verbal and emotional abuse, but I think there's got to be a way to do it.

Several women called for breaking up the good ol' boy network that protected offenders. Hiring more female police officers was another common suggestion. This interviewee, like some others, saw such a change as an effective means of breaking up the good ol' boy network:

Put more women on the force, because men have no compassion in these kinds of cases. Cops are number one bad for unwanted sex, for forcing unwanted sex on their mates, and they've got to change the whole structure of the protective system with more women on the forces. But when you take a woman on a force that's predominantly men, then they're gonna start thinking like the men do. They've got to change the training in this country on how police treat the public. They treat the public terribly. I mean, I'm not saying in all areas, but in most areas they do not train our policemen to be respectful and polite. They teach them to go in and knock your head off and break your door down. It's Gestapo tactics. And they really need to change the training for and teach these policemen what women are going through, how they are sexually abused by their husbands or anyone. But they don't know. They're all men. How's a man gonna relate to what a woman went through? The only way a person can relate to that is be the same gender and that's why we need more women in that department.

I think when they call a policeman in a sexual attack they should, number one, a woman should go out there—not a man. He should be outside the door in case a man comes around that just raped her or the husband or whoever it is. But the woman is the one that should go in and initially interview. Not a male, because they have no compassion. Men have no compassion. It's a good ol' boys network. And it's terrible that our police have come to that. They're not protection.

Quite a few women joined in the call for more empathetic criminal justice officials. "I know that I would always want to see police and courts be a little more supportive," Peggy said, "a little more, um, a little more of a secure feeling for women and the victims, that the victims feel safer there, instead of them having to argue a corner on the side."

Many battered urban women find courtroom advocates effective sources of social support (Ptacek 1999). Here, we define courtroom advocacy as "the provision of information and support to survivors. It includes exploring with the woman the range, effectiveness and sustainability of options to improve her safety and that of her children. . . . The role of the advocate can be compared to that of a coach, supporting and empowering the woman to attain her goals" (Conlin, Chapman, and Benson 2006, 192).

Unfortunately, such advocates are in short supply in rural areas, and those working there suffer from a lack of funding and are required to travel long distances to help their clients. Rural advocates interviewed by Lewis (2003) reported a need for more people who specialize in sexual assault. Several of our interviewees could not agree more. Jolene was emphatic:

> Advocacy. Advocacy. I think if some people with expertise, some people with experience with these matters, would sit on the front rows of some of the court cases and watch some of this go on and then go to the newspapers you know and have them write up. You know, I sat there and watched domestic violence go through umpteen times and nothing happened. What's gonna happen to them? You know, talk to the person afterwards and ask them, you know, "Do you have any kids?" You know, "Well, what's gonna happen to your kids?" You know, bring those to it. You know, judges don't like that. . . .
>
> That's the only way anything ever gets changed is by people bringing it to attention. Because they can't speak for themselves. It's just like the battered women. Women who are forced to have sex. Those women don't speak for themselves because they can't because they've been beaten down so far that they're afraid to speak for them-

selves. So who gonna speak for them? The guy that's beatin' on 'em? I don't think so!

Another improvement to the criminal justice system that our interviewees recommended was getting rid of the red tape that confronts victims of abuse. One survivor put it in terms of making the system "more efficient" when a woman reports assault. "I know they have a lot of red tape and they have a lot of paperwork and they have a lot of excuses," she said. "Maybe it's not excuses to them, but when it's the person that's the victim, it makes a big difference how they react. If they react slow, then a lot more is gonna happen, lot more's gonna affect the person, the victim. If they would react faster with the law, you know, if it's a crime, it's a crime when it happens and, you know, it's not a crime down the road, and I know the law's the law and they have to do it a certain way."

Opening Up Subsidized Housing

Many women do not or cannot leave abusive partners because they lack the financial means to do so (Conlin, Chapman, and Benson 2006; Sokoloff and Dupont 2005). Furthermore, a sizeable portion of rural women who manage to flee to shelters stay in them only temporarily and return to the "house of horrors" because they cannot afford to rent an apartment or other housing (Sev'er 2002; Tutty 2006; Websdale and Johnson 2005).[3] Subsidized housing is available, but very difficult to acquire. What survivors have to say sensitizes us to the need for more money from state and federal governments to ensure that such women have enough money for food, essential living expenses, and safe housing. Jenny describes a typical situation:

> What's the matter with a little his and her housing? They have all of these subsidized housing developments all over the country. You know, but it's hard to get in as a woman because they don't want a single woman with children especially. They want income verification. They want employment history. They want deposits that women, in my situation at least, didn't have. So there's no place to go, so you have to back home to the guy because usually he's taken all your money. Mine always took mine. He even took my son's

savings—we didn't even know. So make it possible for a woman who has literally nothing but the clothes on her back and interest in protecting herself and her children, make it possible for them to have somewhere to go that has a door with a lock, you know, that's hers and not his.

Respondents' Other Policy Recommendations

The foregoing policy recommendations were those most commonly suggested. Other suggestions include better counseling services, "more safe places to go," and more effective substance abuse programs. A few women mentioned what the literature calls target-hardening measures or access control strategies, such as fences, alarms, and guard dogs—measures that make it difficult for predators to victimize people or places (see Lab 2007).

Or, as Jamie suggested, "to allow them [abused women] to be able, to put them through some kind of self-defense class. If not that, give them something to protect themselves. Give them one of those stingers, something they can use, and don't hold them accountable if they [the perpetrators] get hurt. It is not their [the women's] fault. They are protecting themselves, what they are supposed to do. Like in my situation, I'm sorry, I hope it's not against the law, but I do sleep with a knife. That's my safety. And that is my right as a human to protect myself." Liz recommended the same protective measure:

> Sleep with a knife. I am sorry. But I mean, because there ain't going to be anybody to get you in time to stop it anyway. Or get you one of the kind of guns that zap the crap out of somebody. Sleep with something other than mace, because it ain't all that good. Sleep with a bat or something, and use it. Why should we be held accountable because we busted some guy in the kneecap who was going to rape us? So he lost his knee, oh well. I would rather see that man lose his knee than me to be raped. And when they do bust them for their whatever they have done to somebody, however they have perpetrated somebody, there is nothing more done to them. Why are they just slapped on the hand? If we would stop them after the first person was raped, all these other women who marry into these men, you know, wouldn't have this problem. Know what I am saying?

The rural women interviewed for this study have much in common with survivors in other advanced nations, including Canada, as we have seen (Conlin, Chapman, and Benson 2006). And their recommendations are similar to those made by Robyn Edwards (2004) in her study of issues that face Australian women leaving abusive partners.

New Directions
toward Creative Solutions

Based on data derived from our interviews, our previous empirical work, and a review of the extant literature on separation and divorce sexual assault, some additional policies appear to us appropriate responses to Logan et al.'s (2004) call for the development of creative solutions in rural communities.

The most common reaction to any type of crime in many countries, including the United States, demonstrates what Elliott Currie (1985, 18) refers to as "the tendency to compartmentalize social problems along bureaucratic lines." For example, most North Americans assume that the criminal justice system alone deals with crimes like separation and divorce sexual assault, unrelated to the other parts of society that deal with, that is, fix, the social, economic, and cultural forces that foster the serious violation of legal norms, that is, the forces that cause crime. According to Currie: "The failure to make these necessary connections between causes and consequences stifles the development of intelligent policies to prevent criminal violence, and burdens the criminal justice system with the impossible job of picking up the pieces after broader social policies have done their damage" (1985, 9).

We are not suggesting letting the criminal justice system off the hook. Its response to all types of woman abuse in rural communities cries out for improvement. For example, as Websdale (1998, 194) reminds us: "More has to be done to confront the problem of local police officers being compromised around the enforcement of domestic violence laws. This involves much more than sensitizing and training police officers to handle domestics better. . . . If rural officers are not receiving training in all aspects of enforcing the law at domestics, then they ought to."

Still, the criminal justice system alone can do little, if anything, to address the broader social forces that motivate men to assault women and that preclude women from safely escaping abusive relationships. What is needed is a broader vision.[4] Such an approach involves developing and implementing policies that move the discussion of crime prevention and control out of the realm of criminal justice and into that of social and economic policy (Walker 1998).

Tapping the Public Sector

What can state and federal governments do to improve the plight of rural survivors of separation and divorce sexual assault? Below are three modest proposals: (1) transportation subsidies; (2) job training and education; and (3) increased funding for rural service providers.

SUBSIDIZING TRANSPORTATION. Cars are not luxuries in the three Appalachian research sites selected for this study and in other rural parts of the United States. Rather, they are essential for women's safety and for transport to child care, employment, and support services. Public transportation is not an option in rural communities, so state and federal governments should provide women with money to purchase a car, get insurance, and pay for repairs (Purdon 2003, 49). In Columbus, Ohio, the Transportation Authority subsidizes bus fares; in rural communities, an equal amount of money should be allotted for people who need cars. Similarly, more government money should be used to pay the transportation costs of rural advocates who spend much time on the road in their efforts to save lives.

Much of this support could be provided by mobilizing groups like faith communities, which are especially adept at pooling resources to acquire autos for such women. Campaigns started by public officials could encourage faith groups to collect used cars and to get either donations of money to fix them up, or donations of time from people with the talent to fix them up. This will not solve the problems of purchasing gasoline or insurance, or the problems of groups that wish to withhold cars from women they judge undeserving. Yet it is a start, and with local officials spearheading campaigns (itself a low-cost item), it may be possible to convince each insurance agent to subsidize a couple of women, and each gasoline station to donate a small amount of gas.

SUPPORTING MORE JOB TRAINING AND EDUCATION. As Purdon (2003, 49) contends in her report on woman abuse in rural Ontario, Canada: "More supports and more opportunities for retraining or additional education are needed for abused women so they can find the work that will lead to long-term financial security and independence." However, policy makers should not assume that women who get jobs as a result of state-sponsored education and job training programs will automatically be safe. Some estranged husbands or cohabiting partners engage in "patriarchal terrorism" (Johnson 1995) to humiliate their ex-partners and to make them lose their jobs (DeKeseredy, Alvi, et al. 2003; Raphael 2001; Sokoloff and Dupont 2005). Often, violent means of "sabotaging work efforts" influence employers to fire women to avoid problems in the workplace and to protect coworkers (Conlin, Chapman, and Benson 2006). Hence, it is crucial that policies be created that guarantee abused women the ability to collect unemployment insurance if they cannot work due to injuries sustained from their ex-partners' violent and psychologically abusive behaviors. Legislation is also required to prohibit employers from firing women who are being stalked or assaulted at work (Brandwein 1999).

In addition to ensuring that economically disenfranchised rural women get jobs, they should, like all women, get equal pay for equal work. U.S. women's earnings are between 70 and 75 percent those of men. This is blatantly unfair, and if more women had jobs paying living wages, there would be fewer on welfare and in shelters. Further, more women would work if they had access to affordable, quality child care (DeKeseredy, Alvi, et al. 2003). According to Jensen (2006, 6): "Using TANF flexibility to support home-based child care—more common in rural areas—would help single mothers and dual-worker families."[5]

Job training and education will also prevent many men from engaging in separation and divorce sexual assault and other forms of woman abuse. For example, rural men who lost their farms or jobs in industries such as shoe manufacturing would be much less likely to spend time drinking or doing drugs with their friends if they were given opportunities to achieve meaningful and adequately remunerative employment. Thus, their relationships would more likely to remain intact and they would be much less likely to engage in the harms described in this book, seeking to repair damage to their male identity.

INCREASING FUNDING FOR RURAL SERVICE PROVIDERS. That rural battered women face many barriers to service is due in large part to the lower levels of funding in rural communities compared to urban areas and to the greater efficiency required of rural service providers in using the limited government funds they receive (Lewis 2003). Note, too, that government funding is typically based on number of officially reported sexual assaults. For example, although in Pennsylvania the rural official per capita rate of sexual assault is higher than the urban one, the state allocates Victims of Crime Act funds not on the per capita rate but on absolute numbers (Ruback and Menard 2001). Thus, that most U.S. shelters and rape crisis centers do not provide specific training on wife rape and separation and divorce sexual assault is not the result simply of inadequate preparation or lack of knowledge (Bergen 2006). As Lewis (2003) discovered in her study of sexual assault in the rural United States, rural advocates need more money to hire more advocates and to train them, and they need more money for community outreach. Such increased financial support would improve the quality of services for survivors of separation and divorce sexual assault and ultimately save more lives. As one advocate interviewed by Lewis (2003, 15) put it, "In some sense it all comes down to money."

Renovating Economic Policies

An alarming number of rural people are living "at the razor's edge" (L. Jensen 2006). For example, in 2004, 7.3 million rural U.S. citizens (15.1 percent of the rural population) were living in poverty (Economic Research Council 2004). One of the most salient reasons for this problem is industrial restructuring that reduces jobs, which is related to woman abuse during and after the process of separation and divorce and other variants of male-to-female victimization.

What is to be done? Implementing policies suggested previously, such as state-sponsored child care, would certainly help; however, the private sector also needs to contribute to ongoing efforts to curb poverty and its devastating consequences. One way businesses can achieve this goal is by helping to build a more diverse rural economy through developing and supporting small, community-based businesses and small industrial districts. These initiatives can be created with the help of small business loans, tax incentives, and government–private sector partnerships (Jensen 2006).

Although other strategies are needed to foster economic sustainability, to nourish a community and to develop one that is rich in collective efficacy, jobs and effective social programs are essential (De-Keseredy, Alvi, et al. 2003). What Currie (1985, 263) says about solving the crime problem in urban areas is also directly relevant to rural communities: "In the long run, a commitment to full and decent employment remains the keystone of any successful anticrime policy."

Building Community Capacity

Some researchers, government agencies (e.g., U.S. Department of Housing and Urban Development), and policy analysts argue that Crime Prevention Through Environmental Design (CPTED) can reduce crimes, including violent harms (see Newman 1972). But, as noted by Saville (2004, 1), "there is this persistent belief that CPTED ends at the physical environment; that our responsibility stops by modifying the built environment to reduce crime opportunities." Further, CPTED, in its original form, focused mainly on curbing public crimes in socially and economically disenfranchised urban communities, such as improving the territorial control people have over their buildings (DeKeseredy, Alvi, et al. 2003), and it ignores violence against women behind closed doors. Since the start of the new millennium, however, some international scholars have created a second-generation CPTED that focuses heavily on generating high levels of collective efficacy through community capacity building (Saville and Cleveland 1997).

Again, if there are high levels of collective efficacy in the respondents' communities, they do not function to prevent and deter separation and divorce sexual assault. Thus, informed by examples of how this new variant of CPTED can be modified to help reduce private violence against women in North American urban public housing (see DeKeseredy, Alvi, et al. 2004), we here offer examples of how second-generation CPTED can be tailored to help reduce much pain and suffering in rural areas plagued by poverty, unemployment, isolation, and host of other ills.

Our suggestions also borrow from others' rural CPTED work (DeKeseredy, Donnermeyer, and Schwartz forthcoming) and Liepins's (2000) conception of rural communities as places where people and groups engage in the construction and continuous revision of meanings based on discourses between groups and individuals. These networks represent shifting arrangements of political, economic, and social power within rural communities. We also recognize Oetting and Donnermeyer's (1998) work on the concept of community readiness, that is, the idea that there are levels or stages of relative support for localized interventions and preventive actions. Actions that enhance the readiness of local leaders, including members of law enforcement, to take woman abuse seriously, strengthen other actions that may be undertaken to reduce these forms of violence. In the sections that follow, we build upon the woman abuse scholars' work, plus revised definitions of community and local action. The gender sensitive version of CPTED offered here includes the application of four interrelated strategies that have been developed to address feminist concerns, namely, community culture, connectivity and pro-feminist masculinity, community threshold, and social cohesion (Brassard 2003; Cleveland and Saville 2003; DeKeseredy, Alvi, et al. 2004; DeKeseredy, Donnermeyer, and Schwartz forthcoming).

SHIFTING COMMUNITY CULTURE. This approach calls for the creation of "shared history" in a community through the use of festivals, sporting events, music, and art (Cleveland and Seville 2003). Sometimes referred to as "placemaking" (Adams and Goldbard 2001), this initiative involves the use of plays, concerts, and paintings that send out powerful messages to rural residents about violence against women. Such cultural work, including designing t-shirts to memorialize women's victimization, can occur in such locations as schools, places of worship, county fairs, and community centers, with the assistance of a diverse range of community members.

Although the activities may appear mundane and traditional, perhaps even trivial, their revised context represents one set of strategies for breaking down rural patriarchy and promoting great awareness of woman abuse. In essence, in giving a public voice to the issue, they confront public expressions of rural patriarchy. As well, they increase the readiness of communities to support and sustain actions on a wider scale (Oetting and Donnermeyer 1998), supported by law enforcement, elected officials, and other local elites because it is expedient and in their interest to conform to new standards, rather than to cling tight to anachronistic forms of patriarchy. Shifting community culture in the context of woman abuse in small, rural places addresses directly forms of collective efficacy that facilitate the commission of these offenses and creates new, prosocial forms of collective efficacy that can reduce rapes, beatings, and other abuse.

Graffiti, although offensive to many people, can be constructive and also contribute to placemaking. For example, Ohio University in Athens maintains a concrete wall where students are allowed to paint pictures and murals and write political messages, which are often aimed at promoting social justice. There you will commonly see statements such as "Stop Rape" and "Let's Take Back the Night." Defined by some young people and scholars as "sign painting," such artwork could be done on walls or abandoned barns deemed fit by members of other rural communities; the art would increase the visibility and legitimacy of young and old artistic members of these communities.[6] Perhaps, too, artists could be paid for their work with cash or supplies of spray paint, because many of them are in desperate need of money (Ferrell 1993).

ENCOURAGING CONNECTIVITY AND PROFEMINIST MASCULINITY. Rural residents, like other people, need to connect with members of other communities, as well as groups within their own areas (Cleveland and Saville 2003). Because abused rural women suffer from higher levels of social and geographic isolation than do their urban counterparts (Logan et al. 2004), it is necessary to build easily accessible women's centers in rural communities or very close to them (Hornosty and Doherty 2002). Private and public sector support should create these safe places, which can focus on issues in addition to those related to abuse. For example, like Job Readiness Programs offered in Kentucky woman abuse shelters and with the help of U.S. Department of Labor demonstration grants, women's centers could offer educational programs aimed at training unemployed women for jobs that would contribute to their economic independence.[7] The centers would also be the locus for artistic events and other social activities, as well as provide child care, which gives women time to seek jobs or to get a brief reprieve from the pressures of child rearing.

Apart from providing supportive spaces for women to connect, we need to encourage greater connection among the many men eager to eliminate woman abuse. That we are increasingly seeing "the presence of alternative masculinities incompatible with violence in rural communities" offers hope that "large-scale transformations in the rural gender order are possible over time that may in turn lead to reductions in gendered violence" (Hogg and Carrington 2006, 183). Still, regardless of where they live, most antisexist men do not have opportunities to socialize with other males who are concerned about enhancing women's safety (DeKeseredy, Schwartz, and Alvi 2000). Thus, formal profeminist men's organizations such as the National Organization of Men Against Sexism (NOMAS) should be invited to hold town hall meetings in community centers and other settings where profeminist men can get together and develop individual and collective strategies to reduce woman abuse.

A general point of agreement in the profeminist men's movement is that men must take an active role in stopping woman abuse and eliminating other forms of patriarchal control and domination throughout society. Furthermore, profeminist men place the responsibility for woman abuse squarely on abusive men. A widely cited assertion is that "since it is men who are the offenders, it should be men—not women—who change their behavior" (Thorne-Finch 1992, 236).

Profeminist men like us are involved in an ongoing process of changing themselves, self-examination, and self-discovery (Funk 1993), with the ultimate goal of shedding their "patriarchal baggage" (Thorne-Finch 1992). Katz (2006, 260) refers to this process as "similar to the sort of introspection required of antiracist whites." Such profeminist men continue to make great strides in their day-to-day life to escape from the "man box" and to move from being simply "well-meaning men" to becoming profeminist men. The "man box," a term created by Tony Porter (2006b), holds the following elements of "hegemonic masculinity" (Connell 1995): avoid all things feminine; restrict one's emotions severely; show toughness and aggression; strive for achievement and status; exhibit nonrelational attitudes toward sexuality; "measure up to the patriarchal view of the ideal masculine body"; and actively engage in homophobia (Levant 1994; Messerschmidt 2000, 93).

According to Porter (2006a, 1), a well-meaning man is "a man who believes women should be respected. A well-meaning man would not assault a woman. A well-meaning man, on the surface, at least, believes in equality for women, a well-meaning man believes in women's rights. A well-meaning man honors the women in his life. A well-meaning man, for all practical purposes, is a nice guy, a good guy."

However, by remaining silent, well-meaning men directly or indirectly collude with abusive men. As Ted Bunch (2006, 1) points out: "When we remain bystanders we are making a choice to support the abuse. The abusive behavior by any man reflects and therefore reinforces the established status and privileges of all men."

Profeminist men are very vocal about ending male privilege, woman abuse, and other highly injurious symptoms of patriarchy. Further, they work individually and collectively to change men by criticizing and challenging through other means the broader social and economic structure and institutions like the pornography industry, the military, the media, professional sports, and the criminal justice system (Kimmel and Mosmiller 1992; Thorne-Finch 1992). For example, profeminist men boycott strip clubs, confront men who make sexist jokes and who abuse their female partners, support and participate in woman abuse awareness programs, and express their views by supporting and voting for local officials who believe the same and are ready and willing to implement policies and actions that break down rural patriarchy related to violence against women (DeKeseredy, Donnermeyer, and Schwartz forthcoming).

What is especially impressive about profeminist men is that they recognize that the most effective means of prevention and intervention are at the social and cultural systems levels. Alcoholics Anonymous functions in a similar way and has many successful outcomes. For example, we know from the rural study described in this book that one of the most important factors in facilitating separation/divorce sexual assault and other types of woman abuse is a support system built up of pro-abuse men. AA replaces prodrinking peers with those who oppose drinking (social system intervention) and replaces prodrinking norms, values, and beliefs with the opposite set of norms, values, and beliefs (cultural system intervention) (Bowker 1998). Likewise, profeminist masculinism replaces pro-abuse peers with antisexist peers and patriarchal norms, values, and beliefs with those that are profeminist (DeKeseredy, Schwartz, and Alvi 2000).

Rural progressive men's groups can also discuss how and where male members can apply for jobs, effective job interview strategies, and ideas for running a small local business. Initiatives such as these, according to proponents of second-generation CPTED, bring people together "in common purpose" (Cleveland and Saville 2003) and connect them with outside groups that can help them acquire financial and other forms of support for peacemaking efforts. Outside groups also help people avoid reinventing the wheel. For example, established women's groups (e.g., the Ohio Domestic Violence Network located in Columbus) and male anti-sexist collectives (e.g., A Call to Men based in Charlotte, North Carolina) in other communities can share existing sets of best practices that can be tailored to meet a new group's needs and quickly implemented at little or no financial cost.

ENHANCING THE COMMUNITY THRESHOLD.   Enhancing the community threshold involves reducing fear of crime. Except for violent street crime, many rural citizens and urban dwellers have the same concerns about crime (Weisheit, Falcone, and Wells 2006). Some researchers argue that fear of crime may be increased in rural communities by low levels of policing, the absence of streetlights, and perceived dangers posed by members of other ethnic groups moving into traditionally all-white areas (Hogg and Carrington 2006; Lawtey and Deane 2001). Fear of crime in public places influences many women to stay indoors, which makes it even more difficult for them to obtain knowledge about services avail-able to abused women and to develop social ties with neighbors who might be willing to confront the men who assault them in their homes or elsewhere (DeKeseredy and MacLeod 1997).

In North America, vandalism is a powerful determinant of women's fear of crime in rural areas, just as in public housing estates (Donnermeyer 2006; Donnermeyer and Phillips 1982, 1984).[8] In fact, a key finding of studies of collective efficacy by Sampson, Raudenbush, and Earls (1997) is that in neighborhoods of concentrated disadvantage that band together for informal social control, community threshold can be enhanced and violent crimes can be reduced; they can also pool their collective power to extract from local agencies such resources as garbage collection and housing code enforcement. For example, not only do high-tech security devices not reduce crime in public housing, but also they offer one more expensive item to vandalize (James 1997). However, in Melbourne, Australia, for example, provisions for tenant empowerment had a major effect on both crime and fear. When a responsive management system is put into place (including tenant management) and combined with tenant decision making in security measures, sharp reductions in women's fear of public places are possible.

Thus, strategies aimed at reducing women's fear, increasing perceptions of safety in public housing estates, and making women feel comfortable leaving their homes do not require a major criminal justice response. Instead, they may involve tenant empowerment around issues related to garbage, noise, vandalism, and people who drink and do drugs in public places (Alvi et al. 2001). What works in public housing estates may also work in rural communities. In fact, rural social order has traditionally been maintained through informal rather than formal processes of social control (e.g., policing) (Weisheit, Falcone, and Wells 2006). So some researchers contend that to prevent vandalism, rural residents should get together to take action, such as maintaining and cleaning structures that have no apparent usefulness, taking such inexpensive measures as Holland (2006, 2) recommends in a paper on rural vandalism protection:

Keep the grass mowed and the surrounding sidewalks free of weeds and rocks.

Maintain the integrity of doors and windows and use sturdy locks.

Soap all the windows. If the structure is in an isolated area, neatly cover all windows with plywood or some other protective material.

Inspect for and remove bird nests and other material that represents a fire hazard.

Take steps to prevent unauthorized entry through ventilation ports, etc.

BUILDING SOCIAL COHESION. All communities, even small ones, are composed of complex networks of people (Liepins 2000; Oetting and Donnermeyer 1998), and reducing woman abuse and other violent crimes in rural communities requires building social cohesiveness and hence tapping into these networks, as forms of social cohesion, at strategic places (Lee 2008). Second-generation CPTED studies show that teaching positive communication skills and conflict resolution enhances community cohesiveness (Gilligan 2001; Saville and Clear 2000). In many rural communities, schools represent strategic places for such work, as they are the primary social centers for all members, young and old (DeKeseredy, Donnermeyer, and Schwartz forthcoming). To reduce

---

6.1 KEY CHARACTERISTICS OF HEALTHY RELATIONSHIPS

- Listening to each other.
- Feeling good about yourself.
- Having fun together.
- Trusting each other.
- Can talk about your feelings.
- Trying to work things out.
- Feeling equal to each other.
- Wanting to have sex.
- Feeling safe having sex.
- You both agree on birth control and on safer-sex protection.

Source: Victoria Women's Sexual Assault Centre 1994, 22.

---

woman abuse in rural communities, then, schools should build empathy into the curriculum through constant attention to the intersections of race, gender, and class, and require students to take on the role or point of view of the "other" (Connell 1995; De Keseredy, Schwartz, and Alvi 2000; Messerschmidt 2000). Further, in local schools, town halls, or other central meeting places, workshops could be given designed to train people specifically what to do when confronted with male-to-female violence in public places and behind closed doors. Participants should also be taught how to support victims to seek help in appropriate ways and to work to help abusive men become peaceful (Hazler 1996). Along similar lines, prisons across the United States are using violent offenders to train dogs, under the theory that providing offenders with a dependent animal that gives love and attention will help them empathize with others. Rural communities might consider such imaginative ideas.

To supplement school programs, booklets such as *Today's Talk about Sexual Assault* should be distributed to teenage girls throughout rural areas. Developed in British Columbia, Canada, by the Victoria Women's Sexual Assault Center (VWSAC), the *Today's Talk* booklet helps girls recognize the difference between healthy and unhealthy relationships, and includes a wealth of practical information on other issues, such as sexual assault and AIDS (see boxes 6.1 and 6.2).

6.2 KEY CHARACTERISTICS OF UNHEALTHY RELATIONSHIPS

- One person has more power than the other.
- There is jealousy and possessiveness.
- You don't listen to each other.
- You feel bad about yourself.
- One or both partners try to control the other.
- You feel criticized or picked on.
- You don't trust each other.
- There is pressure to stay in the relationship.
- You are forced to have sex.
- There is a lot of anger, fighting, or violence.
- You can't talk about your feelings.

Source: Victoria Women's Sexual Assault Centre 1994, 22.

The VWSAC booklet and others like it advise teenage girls how to avoid abusive boys. However, as stated by profeminist men, because it is men who are the abusers, shouldn't it be they who change their attitudes, beliefs, and behaviors? If men are the primary perpetrators of intimate violence, shouldn't there be programs, videos, booklets, and the like designed to prevent them from beating, raping, and psychologically abusing women? Not surprisingly, the VWSAC booklet's strategies specifically tailored for boys are just as appropriate for older males. Consider these examples:

- Accept the fact that no means no. If a girl tells you that she doesn't want to have sex, STOP.
- Don't try to read your girlfriend or dating partner's mind. Rather, ask her what she wants. She may just want to be close and cuddle; this is not the same as wanting to have sexual intercourse.
- Listen to other guys and how they talk about women. Ask yourself how you feel about what they say. Are these guys respectful or not? Decide for yourself if you want to be part of the conversation. Being male doesn't mean you have to talk tough. (VWSAC 1994, 300–331)

THE PROMISE OF CRIME PREVENTION THROUGH ENVIRONMENTAL DESIGN. Three decades of first-generation CPTED rarely, if ever, addressed woman abuse in private settings (Saville 2004). Certainly, the same can be said about the bulk of work being done on second-generation CPTED. This is not to say, however, that this approach cannot be tailored to deal with woman abuse in intimate relationships. Indeed, it has been modified to address the plight of poor women in urban public housing communities, as we have seen, and we agree with DeKeseredy, Donnermeyer, and Schwartz (forthcoming) that a gendered second-generation CPTED could help make a difference in rural communities.

Donnermeyer, Jobes, and Barclay's (2006, 212) assertion that "rural crime can be most effectively . . . understood through the organizing concept of community" heavily informs the application of the four modified principles of second-generation CPTED we have just outlined. Still, the initiatives we proposed are not exclusively those of CPTED. Policy analysts influenced by different criminological schools of thought, such as feminism, have suggested similar strategies. Will they work? This is an empirical question that can be answered only empirically. Perhaps for now sociologist Paul Jargowsky (1997, 213) has the best answer: "The task is difficult and the results of even our best efforts are uncertain, but to continue our current path is to give the wrong answer to Martin Luther King's question: 'Where do we go from here—chaos or community?'" Policy makers, researchers, and the general public, we hope, will choose community.

SUMMARY

This book broadens the focus of separation and divorce sexual assault theory and research. Furthermore, our project contributes to the expansion of rural crime research. Above all, the exploratory qualitative data presented in this book support Lewis's (2003) assertion that there are many hidden acts of sexual violence in U.S. rural communities that are often ignored. Still, much more empirical and theoretical work on these issues is needed. The policies proposed by forty-three rural Ohio women and us are not the only effective solutions. Rather, they are key elements of much-needed community-based, collaborative efforts. Policy development must also be highly sensitive to the ways in which broader social forces contribute to the harms identified in this book. Achieving this goal is a challenge, given many people's reluctance to foster major social change. And as Websdale (1998, 194) discovered in his study of woman battering in rural Kentucky, "any social policy initiatives must use the structure of rural patriarchy, in all its intricate manifestations, as an essential frame of reference."

The bulk of this book focused on terrifying examples of what happens to some rural women when they want to leave, try to leave, or have left their marital or cohabiting partners. Their voices tell us much about gender relations, motives, thoughts, and human feelings (Goetting 1999). Still, while they were brutalized during and after attempts to leave their partners, they were "battered, but not beaten."[9] They are survivors with plans for the future, and we end this chapter with examples of their "triumph against all odds" (Sev'er 2001).

Many women plan to continue their education. Joanie "would like a Ph.D. in plasma physics," and Martie stated, "I'm really trying to concentrate more on, um, uh, finishing my graduate degree."

Reestablishing relations with their children came up in conversations with many women, a plan that is crucial for their own lives and mental health (Sev'er 2002). As Joan said, "I haven't had much relationship with my children the past few years, so I want to get that back on track." Samantha plans to "visit with my kids and just try to get back to myself."

Other women we talked to plan to get jobs, continue going to counselors, become advocates, and acquire enough money to purchase their own home. These and other moving examples of survival warrant much celebration, given that many of the forty-three women could have easily been killed and some still face the threat of homicide. When we asked Mary about her life since escaping an abusive ex-partner, she said: "I have never been so excited in my life. You know, how many people get a second chance? I nearly died two years ago, several times, and my kids are now home and not many people get a second chance like I do. I really want this to work out."

Appendix A.
Separation/Divorce Sexual Assault Screen Questions

Date of Interview: ___/ ___/ ___
                   M   D   Y

Time of Interview: _____

When you receive a call, read the following preamble to the screen questions:
Hello, Mae (or Carolyn) speaking. Thank you for calling. How are you today? Are you interested in our study?

If they express an interest in the study, say the following:
As you know, two of my Ohio University colleagues and I are conducting a study of women's unwanted sexual experiences when they wanted to end or have ended relationships with their husbands or live-in male partners. Our research is sponsored by a grant provided by the U.S. Department of Justice and the results will be used to help make women's lives safer.

I just need to ask you a few brief questions to make sure that you are eligible to participate in our study. Any information you give me will be carefully protected and held as confidential. No one will ever be able to identify you because of your answers. Also, you don't have to answer any question you don't want to answer.

Before I ask *you* some questions, do you have any questions you want to ask *me*?
(Be prepared for them to ask you, "What do you mean by unwanted sex?" If they do, provide them with our broad definition.

If the respondent wants to verify the study, tell her that she can call Jo Ellen Sherow, Ohio University's director of research compliance at (740) 593–0664.)

If the respondent doesn't have any questions for you, proceed to ask the following questions:

1. Is it safe for you to talk now? *(If not, please ask the respondent to call back at a time that is safe for her.)*
2. How old are you? _____ *(If the respondent is under 18, please thank her for her time and politely tell her that she is ineligible to participate in the study. Also, ask if she would like to ask you any questions.)*
3. How did you find out about our study? *(Note how she found out on your resource table.)*
4. In which county do you live? *(Note this information for help coding subsequent interview.)*
5. Have you ever been married or lived with a male partner?

   Yes

   No

   (If a respondent says no, thank her for her time and politely tell her that she is ineligible to participate in the study. Also, ask if she would like to ask you any questions.)

Those who answered "yes" should then be asked the next set of questions. Before you ask them, read the following preamble:
Many women experience a wide range of unwanted sexual experiences when they want to end or have ended a relationship with their husbands or live-in male partners. Their experiences could have occurred anywhere and at any time and don't always involve physical force. Also, unwanted sexual experiences could occur while women are awake, asleep, unconscious, drunk, or otherwise incapacitated.

   I realize that it may be difficult to discuss your own unwanted sexual experiences, but if I may, I would like to ask you a few sensitive questions. You only have to answer "yes" or "no" to most of these questions and again, all your answers will be completely confidential. *(Read each question to the respondent and circle the response category that best represents her answer.)*

6. At any time in your life, did your husband or a live-in male partner ever *try* to make you have unwanted sex when you wanted to leave him or after you left him? *(Be prepared for respondents asking you to clarify what you mean by "try." Give examples if necessary.)*

   Yes

   No

7. At any time in your life, did your husband or live-in male partner ever *make* you have unwanted sex when you wanted to leave him or after you left him? *(Be prepared for respondents asking you to clarify what you mean by "make." Give examples if necessary.)*

    Yes

    No

Respondents who answered "yes" to one or both of these questions should then be asked the next question. If they answered "no" to both questions, go to Question 8.

8. Is your husband or live-in male partner still making or trying to make you have unwanted sex with him because you want to end or have ended the relationship?

    Yes

    No

9. I really appreciate the time you have taken to talk to me. And I'd like to again assure you that everything you said will remain strictly confidential.

    I realize that the topics covered in our study are sensitive and that many women don't want to talk about their unwanted sexual experiences. But I'm also a bit worried that I haven't asked the right questions.

    Is there anything you would like to tell me that's important that I have not asked? *(Below, write down the respondent's experiences if they are acts of unwanted sex that occurred while she was either planning to end, trying to end, in the process of ending, or after she ended her relationship with a husband or live-in romantic male partner.)*

_____

_____

_____

_____

_____

_____

_____

_____

_____

_____

_____

Respondents who answered "yes" to Question 5 or 6, or who provided relevant experiences in response to Question 8, should be told the following:
Thank you very much for your help with this project. I fully realize that you have had some very bad experiences and we do want to help to make women's lives safer. So, I would greatly appreciate your participation in another confidential face-to-face interview at either a safe Ohio University office or at another safe location of your choosing. My interview will take one or two hours and will be scheduled at your convenience. I will pay you $25.00 in cash for your time and 31 cents per mile for your transportation costs. Would you like to be interviewed?

If she says "yes," then set up a time and location, ask her if she would like to ask you any questions and thank her for her help. If she says that she needs to think about it, then ask her to call you back at her convenience (give her your cell phone number), thank her for her help, and ask her if she would like to ask you any questions.

If a respondent answered "no" to Questions 5 and 6 and did not provide any relevant sexual assault information in response to Question 8, thank her for her time and politely tell her that while you greatly appreciate her taking the time to talk to you, she is ineligible to participate in our study. Also, ask her if she would like to ask you any questions.

Regardless of whether respondents are eligible to be interviewed or want to be interviewed, be prepared for all of them to ask you where they can go for help. If they do, please give them the names of local support services and their telephone numbers. Some respondents might also ask for the addresses of local support services, which you will provide upon request.

Appendix B.
Semi-Structured Interview Schedule

General Background Questions

First, I would like to ask you some general background questions. Again, I can't emphasize enough that everything you tell me will be kept completely confidential and no one will ever be able to identify you with your answers.

1. I realize that I asked you this before, but I would like to make sure that I have the right information. How did you find out about this study?
2. How old are you?
3. In which county do you live?
4. How long have you lived there?
5. Do you live in or near a city or town, or do you live far away from the nearest town or city?
6. Is transportation a problem for you? In other words, can you get to where you want to go whenever you want or need to?
7. Right now, are you employed full- or part-time? *(If she says "yes," ask her what she does. If she is not working then ask her how she tries to make ends meet.)*
8. About how much money did you live on in 2002?
9. What is the highest level of education you have completed?
10. Have you ever been married or have you ever lived with a male romantic partner? *(If she answers "no," thank her for her time and politely tell her that she is ineligible to participate in this study. Pay her for her time and reimburse her for her travel expenses. Then ask her if she has any questions and give her a list of support services.)*

11. Are you currently married or living with a male romantic partner? *(If she says "no," ask her if she is legally or unofficially separated, divorced, or widowed. If she says "yes," ask her about her partner's job status, yearly income, and education level.)*
12. Do you have any children?
13. Have you raised or helped raise someone else's child or children?
14. Do you consider yourself as belonging to any particular ethnic or racial group? *(If she says "yes," ask her which group she belongs to.)*
15. What country were you born in? *(If she was not born in the U.S., ask her where she was born and if she is an immigrant or a refugee from another country.)*
16. Do you have a religious affiliation?

PERCEPTIONS OF SAFETY

The next questions are about how safe you generally feel at home and in your community.

17. How much of a problem do you think there is with *crime* in your community?
18. How safe do you generally feel being alone in public places in your community?
19. How safe do you generally feel when you are at home?
20. Do you feel safer alone at home or when someone else is with you?
21. What about women experiencing *unwanted sex* . . . do you think this is a big problem in your community, some problem, or almost no problem? *(Probe: Can you elaborate on that?)*
22. Do you think *rape or sexual assault* is a big problem in your community, some problem, or almost no problem? *(Probe: Can you elaborate on that?)*

SOCIAL NETWORK

The next questions are about your relations with neighbors, friends, and other members of your community.

23. How often do you get together with friends in your community in a typical week?
24. How often do you get together with your neighbors in a typical week?

25. Could you count on your neighbors to help you solve your personal problems?

26. Could you count on friends in your community to help you solve your personal problems?

27. Have you *personally* known *any* women who've been raped or sexually assaulted? *(If she says "yes," ask her to tell you how many.)*

UNWANTED SEXUAL EXPERIENCES

Many women in Ohio and other parts of the U.S. experience a wide range of unwanted sexual experiences when they want to end or have ended a relationship with their husbands or live-in male partners. Their experiences could have occurred anywhere and at any time and don't always involve force. Also, unwanted sexual experiences could occur while women are awake, asleep, unconscious, drunk, or otherwise incapacitated.

I realize that it may be difficult to discuss your own unwanted sexual experiences, but if I may, I would like to ask you some sensitive questions.

Feel free to stop me at any time, and if you feel uncomfortable with a question, please let me know.

28. At any time in your life, did your husband or live-in male partner ever *try* to make you have unwanted sex when you wanted to leave him or after you left him? *(If she says "yes," ask her what happened and ask her if it happened often. Also, be prepared for respondents to ask you to clarify what you mean by "unwanted sex" and by the term "try." If she says "no," skip to Question 32.)*

29. When did it happen?

30. Why do you think he (or they) did this?

31. In addition to trying to make you have unwanted sex, did this man (or these men) ever hurt you in other ways? *(Probe: Destroying your prized possessions, hit you, emotionally hurt you, or hurt your pets or children?)*

32. At any time in your life, did your husband or live-in male partner ever *make* you have unwanted sex when you wanted to leave him or after you left him? *(If she says "yes," ask her what happened and ask her if it happened often. Also, be prepared for respondents to ask you to clarify what you mean by the term "make." If she says "no," skip to Question 36.)*

33. When did it happen?

34. Why do you think he (or they) did this?
35. In addition to making you have unwanted sex, did this man (or men) ever hurt you in other ways? *(Probe: Destroying your prized possessions, hit you, emotionally hurt you, or hurt your pets or children?)*
36. Did the man (or men) who tried and/or made you have unwanted sex when you wanted to leave or after you left him ever look at pornography?
37. Did the man (or men) who tried and/or made you have unwanted sex when you wanted to leave or after you left him ever make you look at pornography?
38. Did he (or did they) spend a lot of time with his male friends? *(If she says "yes," ask her to tell you what he usually did or does with his friends.)*
39. Does he (or did they) have friends who hit women or who sexually assault them?
40. Does he (or do they) feel that men should be in charge at home?
41. Did he (or they) use drugs or alcohol before he (or they) tried and/or made you have unwanted sex with him (or them)?
42. Did he (or they) try to or make *you* use drugs or alcohol before he (or they) tried or made you have unwanted sex with him (or them)?
43. Are there other things you would like to tell me about the man (or men) who tried or made you have unwanted sex that you think are important?

CONSEQUENCES OF UNWANTED
SEPARATION/DIVORCE SEXUAL ASSAULT

Now, I would like to ask you a question about the effects of your unwanted sexual experiences.

44. How much effect did your unwanted sexual experiences have on your life? *(Probe: Emotional, physical, economic, sexual effects?)*

EXPERIENCES WITH SOCIAL SUPPORT PROVIDERS

Some people turn to others for help stopping or dealing with unwanted sexual experiences that occurred when they wanted to end or have ended a relationship with their husbands or live-in male partners. We would like to know about the help you asked for and/or received.

45. Do you feel different from other women who have experienced unwanted sex or other types of abuse?
46. Did you turn to anyone for help? *(If she says "yes," ask her who she turned to and ask her how satisfied she was with the help she received. If she says "no," ask her why she didn't turn to anyone for help and then go to the questions about survivors' policy recommendations in the next section.)*
47. Who gave you the best help and did their support make you safer?
48. Who gave you the worst help? *(Ask her to elaborate.)*

SURVIVORS' POLICY RECOMMENDATIONS

As you know, we want to make women's lives safer. So, now we would like to know what you think are the best ways of preventing women from experiencing unwanted sex when they want to leave or have left their husbands or live-in male partners. We would also like to know what you think could be done to improve the criminal justice system's response to problems like yours.

49. What do you think is the most effective way of preventing unwanted sex during and after separation/divorce?
50. How can the criminal justice system be more helpful to survivors of unwanted sex during and after separation/divorce?
51. How can other types of social support, such as shelters, counselors, your friends, etc., be more helpful to survivors of unwanted sex during and after separation/divorce?
52. What would you do if you were in charge of developing policies aimed at preventing unwanted sex during and after separation/divorce in your community?
53. What advice would you give to other women who have had unwanted sexual experiences when they wanted to leave or have left their husbands or male live-in partners?

PLANS FOR THE FUTURE

54. What are your plans for the future?
55. What is your biggest concern right now? *(Probe: Are you most concerned about your safety, legal issues, finding a place to live, money, etc.?)*

CONCLUSION

56. Is there anything else you would like to tell me that's important that
    I have not asked about?
57. Are there any questions you would like to ask me?

Thank you for your time and effort. I greatly appreciate your help and I
hope that the information you gave me will help make women's lives
safer. Please feel free to call me if you have any questions or have some
concerns.

Notes

Chapter 1   Introduction: The Dark Side
of the Heartland

Epigraph: To maintain confidentiality, we have changed all the names of the women who participated in the study described in this book and who are quoted throughout.

1. Stephen Lewis is cofounder and codirector of AIDS-Free World, a new international AIDS advocacy organization based in the United States. He was Canada's ambassador to the United Nations from 1984 to 1988.

2. Since 1990, studies on crime and its control in rural areas have proliferated (Donnermeyer, Jobes, and Barclay 2006). However, the bulk of the research does not focus on the plight of women abused by male intimates.

3. These elements are residential instability, family disruption, and ethnic heterogeneity.

4. To the best of our knowledge, one would be hard-pressed to find an entire chapter or section on rural crime in any best-selling U.S. criminology text. Such selective inattention is also evident in Canadian and Australian texts (Scott, Barclay, and Donnermeyer 2007).

5. Some studies show that rural masculinities are "less heterogeneous and more heteronormative" than are urban masculinities (Carrington 2007).

6. Between 50 and 90 percent of battered women in the United States try to leave abusive relationships (Block 2003; K. Davis 1999; DeKeseredy and Joseph 2003; Horn 1992; Stark 2007).

7. We define intimate femicide as "the killing of females by male partners with whom they have, have had, or want to have, a sexual and/or emotional relationship" (Ellis and DeKeseredy 1997, 592).

8. Similar to French sociologist Emile Durkheim's (1964) view of rural life as "mechanical solidarity," late nineteenth-century German sociologist Ferdinand Tonnies's (1940) work on urbanism spawned the concept of "gemeinschaft," a term now widely used in sociology. Briefly, Tonnies argued that, on the one hand, in traditional, rural, or gemeinschaft societies, people have strong attachments to each other. He conceptualizes modern, urban, gesellschaft societies, on the other hand, as the "antithesis" of gemeinschaft because they are tenuous, impersonal, and heterogeneous (Donnermeyer, Jobes, and Barclay 2006; Fagen 2005).

9. Of the 229 men in Bergen and Bukovec's (2006) sample, 76 percent used such emotional coercion to have sex with their female partners.

10. A study of rural South African men found that rapes of nonpartners were

associated with elements of male peer support, such as criminal gang membership and perceived peer pressure to have sex (Jewkes et al. 2006).
11. See Sokoloff 2005 for in-depth reviews of research on violence against women from diverse racial/ethnic and socioeconomic backgrounds.

CHAPTER 2   THINKING THEORETICALLY ABOUT SEPARATION
AND DIVORCE SEXUAL ASSAULT

1. "Prevalence" refers to the percentage of women who reported ever having experienced separation and divorce sexual assault.
2. See DeKeseredy and Perry 2006a; Lynch, Michalowski, and Groves 2000; and Schwartz and Hatty 2003 for recent in-depth overviews of these and other variants of critical criminological thought.
3. This is a modified version of Jock Young's (1988) definition of radical criminology.
4. Studies that focused on gender issues included DeKeseredy and Joseph 2006; Gagne 1992; Krishnan, Hilbert, and Pase 2001; Miller and Veltkamp 1989; Navin, Stockum, and Campbell-Ruggaard 1993; and Websdale 1995, 1998.
5. As pointed out by many scholars and activists, the first question blames females for the abuse they endure in intimate relationships. And, as Stark (2007, 130), and others frequently note: "It is men who stay, not their partners." Indeed, "there is no greater challenge in the abuse field than getting men to exit from abusive relationships" (see also, e.g., Bancroft 2002).
6. This model is also informed by perspectives offered by DeKeseredy and Schwartz 1993, 2002; Ellis and DeKeseredy 1997; and Wilson and Daly 1992.
7. Note that some researchers (e.g., Dutton 2006) who make this claim also call for marginalizing the consideration of gender in the etiology of violence against women. See DeKeseredy and Dragiewicz's (2007) feminist response to this call.
8. There is a propensity for many male psychiatrists to blame female victims for their male partners' abusive behavior (Stark 2007).
9. The CTS was developed by Straus (1979) to study violence within families. Applied to intimate partner violence, this measure and the recently developed CTS2 (Straus et al. 1996) solicit information from men and women about the various tactics they used to resolve conflicts in their relationships. Most versions of the CTS consist of at least eighteen items that measure three different ways of handling interpersonal conflict in intimate relationships: reasoning, verbal aggression (referred to by some researchers as psychological abuse), and violence. The CTS has been criticized on several grounds, including its inability to measure the contexts, meanings, and motives of violence (DeKeseredy 2006; DeKeseredy and Schwartz 2003).
10. See Schwartz and DeKeseredy 1997 for an in-depth review of sociological research on gang rapes committed by college students.
11. See Bachar and Koss 2001; DeKeseredy 2005; and Mahoney, Williams, and West 2001 for reviews of studies of the incidence and prevalence of woman abuse.
12. A husband is exempt in these states if his wife is mentally or physically impaired, unconscious, asleep, or unable to consent (Bergen 2006).
13. See DeKeseredy 1990; DeKeseredy and Schwartz 1998a, 2002, 2005; and

Schwartz and DeKeseredy 1997 for in-depth reviews of the sociological literature on the relationship between male peer support and woman abuse.

14. Similar ethnographic data were uncovered in rural South Africa. For example, Wood and Jewkes (2001) discovered that among male peers, sexual conquests were regarded as a sign of status, "whether achieved by wooing, begging, trickery, or, ultimately, the use of force" (Jewkes et al. 2006, 2950).

15. See Miller and Schwartz 1992 and Schwartz and DeKeseredy 1997 for more detailed analyses of the relationship between male peer support and the commodification of women through sexual objects.

16. Most North American studies of male rapists, regardless of whether they focused on male peer support, were conducted on college campuses (Bachar and Koss 2001; Jewkes et al. 2006).

CHAPTER 3 THE STUDY: DOING FEMINIST RESEARCH
IN THE HEARTLAND

1. Positivism assumes that human behavior is determined and can be measured (Curran and Renzetti 2001). And, as John Hagan (1985, 78) correctly points out, within the discipline of criminology, there is "an enduring commitment to measurement." At the time we wrote this chapter, Claire Renzetti held the prestigious position of editor of *Violence against Women: An International and Interdisciplinary Journal.*

2. See DeKeseredy 2007a for a biographical account of how he became a feminist man and how he does his empirical, theoretical, and political work on woman abuse.

3. See DeKeseredy, Alvi et al. 2003 for more information on the public housing study.

4. Logan et al. (2006) found that significantly more rural than urban women who participated in their stalking study stated that they were scared that a stalker would kill them.

5. Other studies of rural woman abuse discovered the same problem with lack of anonymity (e.g., Gagne 1992; Grama 2000; Websdale 1998).

6. Among the researchers, Karen Bachar, Raquel Kennedy Bergen, Mary Koss, and Claire Renzetti devoted a substantial amount of time and effort to helping us develop this study.

7. There are, however, many challenges to developing partnerships between researchers and practitioners, including time and trust and differences among disciplines. See Edleson and Bible 2001 for an in-depth overview of key issues related to developing and maintaining collaborative research partnerships among social scientists, activists, advocates, practitioners, and abused women.

8. Judith Grant is now based at the University of Ontario Institute of Technology's Faculty of Criminology, Justice, and Policy Studies in Oshawa, Ontario, Canada.

9. The interviewing procedures described here were heavily informed by safety-planning work done by Jill Davies and Eleanor Lyon (1998).

10. These techniques are similar to those used by progressive researchers who conducted the first sweep of the Islington Crime Survey (Jones, MacLean, and Young 1986), a British Study that devoted considerable attention to physical and sexual assaults against women.

11. We never used the term "sexual assault" to recruit participants because our

own research experiences and a review of the extant literature on the measurement of woman abuse (Schwartz 2000), made us concerned that many
women who were sexually assaulted would not necessarily define their victimization this way and thus not participate in our study (Davies and Lyon
1998). Logan et al. (2006, 306) had similar concerns about "common perceptions" of stalking and therefore asked potential participants, "Have you or
someone you know experienced serious conflict or feelings of being controlled in an intimate relationship with a man?"

12. Many researchers now find that giving women money for their time, effort,
and discomfort is the best incentive for participation (Rudy et al. 1994),
although some people claim that paying low-income respondents may be
unethical coercion (Wineman and Durand 1992). However, we felt that paying women was "just compensation for their 'work'" (Campbell and Dienemann 2001, 67).

13. As recommended by leading experts in the field (e.g., Campbell and Dienemann 2001), we asked women we interviewed over the phone for a safe
address to which their checks could be sent. For in-person interviews of
women who have experienced abuse, many researchers prefer public places
such as a university office building, because of the risk of perpetrators "catch-
ing" women being interviewed, resulting in assaults on respondents or interviewers (Campbell and Dienemann 2001). Moreover, perpetrators' friends,
neighbors, or relatives may tell them that a "stranger dropped by the house,"
which could also result in harm to respondents.

14. For example, one of two offices used to conduct interviews had crayons and
some toys, and a research assistant spent time with children of mothers who
were being interviewed in another room.

15. Pilot work for Logan et al.'s (2006) stalking study also revealed that rural communities are more distrustful of researchers and strangers than are urban areas.

CHAPTER 4 EXITING DANGEROUS RELATIONSHIPS: RURAL WOMEN'S EXPERIENCES OF ABUSE AND RISK FACTORS

1. For example, the U.S. VAWS found that 81 percent of the female respondents
who reported being stalked by a husband or ex-husband were also physically
assaulted, and 31 percent stated that they were sexually assaulted (Tjaden and
Thonnes 2000). Other studies reviewed by Logan et al. (2006) show that
stalking that occurs during or after separation/divorce is also associated with
physical, sexual, and psychological abuse.

2. It is estimated that an abusive male partner is seven times more likely to physically assault children (Bancroft 2002; Davies and Lyon 1998; Straus 1983).

3. There is a strong relationship between offenders' alcohol consumption and
intimate femicide (Sharps et al. 2001, 2003).

4. See Schwartz and DeKeseredy 1997 and Schwartz et al. 2001 for more
detailed information on the relationship between all-male sexist conversations, alcohol consumption, and sexual assault on the college campus.

5. For the purpose of this study, we define pornography as "material that com-
bines sex and/or exposure of genitals with abuse or degradation in a manner
that appears to condone or encourage such behavior" (Russell 1998, 3).

6. Given that the consumption of pornography is often a secretive event, it is
possible that many, if not most, of the women in our sample who stated that

their ex-partners did not view pornography were probably unaware of these men's use of pornography (Bergen and Bogle 2000).

7. Gun ownership is strongly related to intimate femicide, especially when intimate partners live apart (Campbell et al. 2003).

8. Illegal drug use was common in our interviewees' communities, in large part because marijuana is the staple crop of many rural Appalachian counties (Clayton 1995; Donnermeyer, Jobes, and Barclay 2006; Weisheit, Falcone, and Wells 2006).

9. Similarly, Sherman's (2005) study of families harmed by the closure of sawmills in a rural California community reveals that some unemployed rural men spent a great deal of time drinking with men in similar situations, and this is one of the key reasons why their wives left or tried to leave them.

CHAPTER 5 THE CONSEQUENCES OF ABUSE
AND WOMEN'S SOCIAL SUPPORT EXPERIENCES

1. The claims regarding rural areas are supported by other rural studies (Booth, Ross, and Rost 1999; DeLeon, Wakefield, and Hagglund 2003; Leukefeld, Clayton, and Myers 1992; Lewis 2003).

2. See Barnett, Miller-Perrin, and Perrin 2005 for an in-depth review of studies of the negative outcomes of various types of violence against women.

3. Other studies have found that many drug-dependent women have experienced various types of woman abuse (Blood and Cornwall 1996; Grant 2006, 2008; Miller and Downs 1993; Raine 2001; Ryan and Popour 1983). Further, some researchers estimate that about 50 percent of all alcoholism in women may be the result of abuse (Davies and Lyon 1998; Hotaling and Sugarman 1986).

4. After nearly seventy years of operation in Nelsonville, Ohio, in 2002 the Rocky Shoes and Boots factory closed and moved to Puerto Rico. None of its sixty-seven displaced workers were offered replacement jobs (Price 2002).

5. See Averill, Padilla, and Clements 2007; Goeckermann, Hamberger, and Barber 1994; Hogg and Carrington 2006; Logan et al. 2004; and Websdale 1998.

6. Another rural study similarly found that abused women rarely sought medical treatment (Bosch and Schumm 2004).

CHAPTER 6 WHERE DO WE GO FROM HERE?
RESEARCH, THEORY, AND POLICY

1. Hogg and Carrington used both quantitative and qualitative methods.

2. "Rural realities" is the title of a quarterly publication of information about trends, issues, and policy alternatives published by the Rural Sociological Society.

3. The phrase is from the title of Sev'er's 2002 *Fleeing the House of Horrors*.

4. "A Broader Vision" is the title of chapter 8 in William Julius Wilson's widely read and cited 1996 book *When Work Disappears: The World of the New Urban Poor*.

5. About three years after the passage of the 1996 Welfare Act in the United States, on October 1, 1999, Temporary Assistance to Needy Families (TANF) regulations increased state flexibility in helping low-income families. States

with large amounts of unused TANF funds may ask to use them for working family supports, including transportation and child care (Stein 1999).

6. As Ferrell (1993) found in his study of Denver graffiti artists, some local business people, homeowners, and others often hire these artists, which fosters their "stake in conformity" (Hirschi 1969), enhances their self-esteem, and contributes to their economic well-being.

7. See Websdale and Johnson 2005 for more information on these programs.

8. See Alvi et al. 2001and Renzetti and Maier 2002 for data derived from studies of women's fear of crime in public housing.

9. We borrow this phrase from Linda MacLeod; it is the title of her 1987 book.

References

Adams, D., and A. Goldbard. 2001. *Creative community: The art of cultural development.* New York: Rockefeller Foundation.

Adler, P. A., and P. Adler. 2003. *Peer power: Preadolescent culture and identity.* New Brunswick, N.J.: Rutgers University Press.

Albrecht, D. E., C. M. Albrecht, and S. L. Albrecht. 2000. Poverty in nonmetropolitan America: Impacts of industrial, employment, and family structure variables. *Rural Sociology* 65:87–103.

Alston, M. 2003. Women's representation in an Australian rural context. *Sociologia Ruralis* 43:474–487.

Alvi, S., W. S. DeKeseredy, and D. Ellis. 2000. *Contemporary social problems in North America.* Toronto: Addison Wesley Longman.

Alvi, S., M. D. Schwartz, W. S. DeKeseredy, and M. O. Maume. 2001. Women's fear of crime in Canadian public housing. *Violence against Women* 7:638–661.

Amato, P. R. 1993. Urban-rural differences in helping friends and family. *Social Psychology Quarterly* 56:249–262.

Anderson, E. 1999. *Code of the street: Decency, violence, and the moral life of the inner city.* New York: Norton.

Appalachian Regional Commission. 2007a. Appalachian region: Economic overview. www.arc.gov/index.do?nodeId=26.

———. 2007b. Regional data results: Socioeconomic data. www.arc.gov/search/LoadQueryData.do?queryId=1andfips=39009.

Archer, J. 2006. Cross cultural differences in aggression between partners. *Personality and Social Psychology Review* 10:133–153.

Arendell, T. 1995. *Fathers and divorce.* Thousand Oaks, Calif.: Sage.

Armstrong, E. A., L. Hamilton, and B. Sweeney. 2006. Sexual assault on campus: A multilevel integrative approach to party rape. *Social Problems* 53:483–499.

Averill, J. B., A. O. Padilla, and P. T. Clements. 2007. Frightened in isolation: Unique considerations for research of sexual assault and interpersonal violence in rural communities. *Journal of Forensic Nursing* 3:42–46.

Bacchetta, P., and M. Power. 2002. Introduction to *Right-wing women: From conservatives to extremists around the world,* ed. P. Bacchetta and M. Power, 1–15. New York: Routledge.

Bachar, K., and M. P. Koss. 2001. From prevalence to prevention: Closing the gap between what we know about rape and what we do. In *Sourcebook on violence against women,* ed. C. M. Renzetti, J. L. Edleson, and R. K. Bergen, 117–142. Thousand Oaks, Calif.: Sage.

Bancroft, L. 2002. *Why does he do that? Inside the minds of angry and controlling men.* New York: Berkley.

Barak, G. 2007. *Violence, conflict, and world order: Critical conversations on state-sanctioned justice.* Lanham, Md.: Rowman and Littlefield.

Barclay, E., J. F. Donnermeyer, and P. C. Jobes. 2004. The dark side of gemeinschaft. *Crime Prevention and Community Safety: An International Journal* 6:7–22.

Barnard, G. W., H. Vera, M. I. Vera, and G. Newman. 1982. Till death do us part: A study of spouse murder. *Bulletin of the American Association of Psychiatry and Law* 10:271–280.

Barnett, O. W., C. L. Miller-Perrin, and R. D. Perrin. 2005. *Family violence across the lifespan: An introduction.* Thousand Oaks, Calif.: Sage.

Barrett, M., and M. McIntosh. 1982. *The anti-social family.* London: Verso.

Bergen, R. K. 1996. *Wife rape: Understanding the response of survivors and service providers.* Thousand Oaks, Calif.: Sage.

———. 2006. Marital rape: New research and directions. *VAWnet*, February, 1–13.

Bergen, R. K., and K. A. Bogle. 2000. Exploring the connection between pornography and sexual violence. *Violence and Victims* 15:227–234.

Bergen, R. K., and P. Bukovec. 2006. Men and intimate partner rape: Characteristics of men who sexually abuse their partners. *Journal of Interpersonal Violence* 21:1375–1384.

Betowski, B. 2007. 1 in 3 boys heavy porn users, study shows. February 23. www.eurekalert.org/pub_releases/2007–02/uoa-oit022307.php.

Black, D. 1983. Crime as social control. *American Sociological Review* 48:34–45.

Block, C. R. 2000. *The Chicago Women's Health Risk Study.* Washington, D.C.: U.S. Department of Justice.

———. 2003. How can practitioners help an abused woman lower her risk of death? *NIJ Journal*, no. 250:4–7.

Block, C. R., and W. S. DeKeseredy. 2007. Forced sex and leaving intimate relationships: Results of the Chicago women's health risk study. *Women's Health and Urban Life* 6:6–23.

Blood, L., and A. Cornwall. 1996. Childhood sexual victimization as a factor in the treatment of substance misusing adolescents. *Substance Use and Misuse* 31:1015–1039.

Bohmer, A., and A. Parrot. 1993. *Sexual assault on the college campus: The problem and the solution.* New York: Lexington.

Booth, B., R. Ross, and K. Rost. 1999. Rural and urban problem drinkers in six southern states. *Substance use and misuse* 34:471–493.

Bosch, K., and W. R. Schumm. 2004. Accessibility to resources: Helping rural women in abusive relationships become free from abuse. *Journal of Sex and Marital Therapy* 30:357–370.

Bourgois, P. 1995. *In search of respect: Selling crack in El Barrio.* New York: Cambridge University Press.

Boyle, T. 2007. Small towns have higher crime rates. *Toronto Star.* June 29.

Bowker, L. H. 1983. *Beating wife-beating.* Lexington, Mass.: Lexington Books.

———. 1998. On the difficulty of eradicating masculine violence: Multisystem overdetermination. In *Masculinities and violence*, ed. L. H. Bowker, 1–14. Thousand Oaks, Calif.: Sage.

Brandwein, R. A. 1999. Family violence, women, and welfare. In *Battered women, children, and welfare reform: The ties that bind*, ed. R. A. Brandwein, 3–16. Thousand Oaks, Calif.: Sage.

Brassard, A. 2003. Integrating the planning process and second-generation CPTED. *CPTED Journal* 2:46–53.

Browning, C. 2002. The span of collective efficacy: Extending social disorganization theory to partner violence. *Journal of Marriage and Family* 64:833–850.

Brownridge, D. A. 2006. Violence against women post-separation. *Aggression and Violent Behavior* 11:514–530.

Brownridge, D. A., and S. S. Halli. 2001. *Explaining violence against women in Canada*. Lanham, Md.: Lexington Books.

Brush, L. D. 1990. Violent acts and injurious outcomes in married couples: Methodological issues in the national survey of families and households. *Gender and Society* 4:56–67.

Buchwald, E., P. R. Fletcher, and M. Roth, eds. 1993. *Transforming a rape culture*. Minneapolis: Milkweed Editions.

Bunch, T. 2006. Ending men's violence against women: A Call to men: National Association of Men and Women Committed to Ending Violence against Women. www.acalltomen.com/page.php?id=52.

Campbell, H. 2000. The glass phallus: Pub(lic) masculinity and drinking in rural New Zealand. *Rural Sociology* 65:562–581.

Campbell, H., and M. M. Bell. 2000. The question of rural masculinities. *Rural Sociology* 65:532–546.

Campbell, J. C., and J. D. Dienemann. 2001. Ethical issues in research on violence against women. In *Sourcebook on violence against women*, ed. C. M. Renzetti, J. L. Edleson, and R. K. Bergen, 57–72. Thousand Oaks, Calif.: Sage.

Campbell, J. C., D. Webster, D. J. Koziol-McLain, C. Block, D. Campbell, M. A. Curry, F. Gary et al. 2003. Risk factors for femicide in abusive relationships: Results from a multisite case control study. *American Journal of Public Health* 93:1089–1097.

Cancino, J. M. 2005. The utility of social capital and collective efficacy: Social control policy in nonmetropolitan settings. *Criminal Justice Policy Review* 16:287–318.

Carastathis, A. 2006. New cuts and conditions for Status of Women Canada. *Toronto Star*, October 11. *www.dominionpaper.ca/canadian_news/2006/10/11new_cuts_a.html*.

Carrington, K. 2007. Violence and the architecture of rural life. In *Crime in rural Australia*, ed. E. Barclay, J. F. Donnermeyer, J. Scott, and R. Hogg, 88–99. Sydney, Aus.: Federation Press.

Claussen, N. 2003. Crisis hotline leads list of mental-health casualties. *Athens News,* May 29.

Clayton, R. R. 1995. *Marijuana in the "third world": Appalachia, U.S.A.* Boulder, Colo.: Lynne Rienner.

Cleveland, G., and G. Saville. 2003. An introduction to 2nd generation CPTED—part 1. *www.cpted.net*.

Conlin, T., J. Chapman, and R. Benson. 2006. *After she leaves: A training and resource manual for volunteers and staff supporting woman abuse survivors and their children during the family law process*. Toronto: Ministry of the Attorney General Ontario Victim Services Secretariat.

Connell, R. W. 1995. *Masculinities*. Berkeley: University of California Press.

Contos Shoaf, L. 2004. *Domestic violence in Appalachian Ohio: The victim's perspective, 2004*. Columbus: Ohio Office of Criminal Justice Services.

Crawford, M., and R. Gartner. 1992. *Woman killing: Intimate femicide in Ontario, 1974–1990*. Toronto: Women We Honor Action Committee.

Cross, P. 2007. Femicide: Violent partners create war zone for women. *Toronto Star,* July 6.

Curran, D. J., and C. M. Renzetti. 2001. *Theories of Crime.* Boston: Allyn and Bacon.

Currie, E. 1985. *Confronting crime: An American challenge.* New York: Pantheon.

———. 1993. *Reckoning: Drugs, the cities, and the American future.* New York: Hill and Wang.

Daly, K., and Chesney-Lind, M. 1988. Feminism and criminology. *Justice Quarterly* 5:497–538.

Davidson, O. G. 1996. *Broken heartland: The rise of America's rural ghetto.* Iowa City: University of Iowa Press.

Davies, J., and E. Lyon. 1998. *Safety planning with battered women: Complex lives / difficult decisions.* Thousand Oaks, Calif.: Sage.

Davis, K. E. (2006). Foreword to T. K. Logan, J. Cole, L. Shannon, and R. Walker, *Partner stalking: How women respond, cope, and survive,* xiii–xv. New York: Springer.

Davis, M. F. 1999. The economics of abuse: How violence perpetuates women's poverty. In *Battered women, children, and welfare reform: The ties that bind,* ed. R. A. Brandwein, 17–30. Thousand Oaks, Calif.: Sage.

DeKeseredy, W. S. 1988. *Woman abuse in dating relationships: The role of male peer support.* Toronto: Canadian Scholars' Press.

———. 1990. Male peer support and woman abuse: The current state of knowledge. *Sociological Focus* 23:129–139.

———. 1995. Enhancing the quality of survey data on woman abuse: Examples from a national Canadian study. *Violence against Women* 1:158–173.

———. 2000. Current controversies on defining nonlethal violence against women in intimate heterosexual relationships: Empirical implications. *Violence against Women* 6:728–746.

———. 2005. Patterns of family violence. In *Families: Changing trends in Canada,* ed. M. Baker, 229–257. Whitby, Ont.: McGraw-Hill Ryerson.

———. 2006. Future directions. *Violence against Women* 12:1078–1085.

———. 2007a. Changing my life among others: Reflections on the life and work of a feminist man. In *Criminal justice diversity: Voices from the field,* ed. S. Miller, 127–145. Boston: Northeastern University Press.

———. 2007b. *Sexual assault during and after separation / divorce: An exploratory study.* Washington, D.C.: U.S. Department of Justice.

———. 2009. Girls and women as victims of crime. In *Women and the criminal justice system: A Canadian perspective,* ed. J. Barker, 315–348. Toronto: Emond Montgomery.

DeKeseredy, W. S., S. Alvi, C. M. Renzetti, and M. D. Schwartz. 2004. Reducing violence against women in public housing: Can second-generation CPTED make a difference? *CPTED Journal* 3:27–37.

DeKeseredy, W. S., S. Alvi, M. D. Schwartz, and E. A. Tomaszewski. 2003. *Under siege: Poverty and crime in a public housing community.* Lanham, Md.: Lexington Books.

DeKeseredy, W. S., J. F. Donnermeyer, and M. D. Schwartz. Forthcoming. Preventing woman abuse in rural communities: The contribution of a gendered second-generation CPTED. *Security Journal.*

DeKeseredy, W. S., J. F. Donnermeyer, M. D. Schwartz, K. Tunnell, and M. Hall. 2007. Thinking critically about rural gender relations: Toward a rural masculinity crisis / male peer support model of separation / divorce sexual assault. *Critical Criminology* 15:295–311.

DeKeseredy, W. S., and M. Dragiewicz. 2007. Understanding the complexities of feminist perspectives on woman abuse: A commentary on Donald G. Dutton's *Rethinking domestic violence. Violence against Women* 13: 874–884.

DeKeseredy, W. S., D. Ellis, and S. Alvi. 2005. *Deviance and crime: Theory, research and policy.* Cincinnati: LexisNexis Anderson.

DeKeseredy, W. S., and W. F. Flack Jr. 2007. Sexual assault in colleges and universities. In *Battleground criminal justice*, ed. G. Barak, 693–697. Westport, Conn.: Greenwood Press.

DeKeseredy, W. S., and C. Joseph. 2003. Understanding separation/divorce sexual assault in rural communities: The contributions of an exploratory Ohio study. Paper presented at the National Institute of Justice Conference on Criminal Justice Research and Evaluation, Washington, D.C.

———. 2006. Separation/divorce sexual assault in rural Ohio: Preliminary results of an exploratory study. *Violence against Women* 12:301–311.

DeKeseredy, W. S., and L. MacLeod. 1997. *Woman abuse: A sociological story.* Toronto: Harcourt Brace.

DeKeseredy, W. S., and B. Perry, eds. 2006a. *Advancing critical criminology: Theory and application.* Lanham, Md.: Lexington Books.

———. 2006b. Introduction to part 1 of *Advancing critical criminology: Theory and application*, ed. W. S. DeKeseredy and B. Perry, 11–17. Lanham, Md.: Lexington Books.

DeKeseredy, W. S., M. Rogness, and M. D. Schwartz. 2004. Separation/divorce sexual assault: The current state of social scientific knowledge. *Aggression and Violent Behavior* 9:675–691.

DeKeseredy, W. S., and M. D. Schwartz. 1993. Male peer support and woman abuse: An expansion of DeKeseredy's model. *Sociological Spectrum* 13:393–413.

———. 1996. *Contemporary criminology.* Belmont, Calif.: Wadsworth.

———. 1998a. Male peer support and woman abuse in postsecondary school courtship: Suggestions for new directions in sociological research. In *Issues in intimate violence*, ed. R. K. Bergen, 83–96. Thousand Oaks, Calif.: Sage.

———. 1998b. *Woman abuse on campus: Results from the Canadian national survey.* Thousand Oaks, Calif.: Sage.

———. 2002. Theorizing public housing woman abuse as a function of economic exclusion and male peer support. *Women's Health and Urban Life* 1:26–45.

———. 2003. Backlash and whiplash: A critique of Statistics Canada's 1999 General Social Survey on Victimization. *Online Journal of Justice Studies.* www.ojjs.icaap.org.

———. 2005. Masculinities and interpersonal violence. In *The handbook of studies on men and masculinities*, ed. M. Kimmel, R. W. Connell, and J. Hearn, 353–366. Thousand Oaks, Calif.: Sage Publications.

———. 2008. Separation/divorce sexual assault in rural Ohio: Survivors' perceptions. *Journal of Prevention and Intervention in the Community* 36:1–15.

DeKeseredy, W. S., M. D. Schwartz, and S. Alvi. 2000. The role of profeminist men in dealing with woman abuse on the Canadian college campus. *Violence against Women* 9:918–935.

DeKeseredy, W. S., M. D. Schwartz, D. Fagen, and M. Hall. 2006. Separation/divorce sexual assault: The contribution of male peer support. *Feminist Criminology* 1:228–250.

DeLeon, P., M. Wakefield, and K. Hagglund. 2003. The behavioral health care needs of rural communities in the 21st century. In *Rural behavioral health care: An inter-*

disciplinary guide, ed. B. Stamm, 23–31. Washington, D.C.: American Psychological Association.

Denham, S. A. 2005a. *Survey conducted by the Appalachian faculty learning community, spring 2004.* Athens, Ohio: Faculty Learning Community, Ohio University.

———. 2005b. *Survey conducted by the Appalachian faculty learning community, spring 2004: Perspectives about stereotypes.* Athens, Ohio: Faculty Learning Community, Ohio University.

———. 2005c. *Voices at Ohio University speak out about Appalachia: Executive report.* Athens: Faculty Learning Community, Ohio University.

Dobash, R. E., and R. Dobash. 1979. *Violence against wives: A case against the patriarchy.* New York: Free Press.

Dobash, R. E., R. P. Dobash, K. Cavanagh, and J. Medina-Ariza. 2007. Lethal and nonlethal violence against an intimate female partner: Comparing male murderers to nonlethal abusers. *Violence against Women*, 13:329–353.

Donnermeyer, J. F. 2006. *Crime and violence in rural communities.* www.ncrel.org/sdrs/areas/issue/envrnmnt/drugfree/v1donner.htm.

Donnermeyer, J. F., P. Jobes, and E. Barclay. 2006. Rural crime, poverty, and community. In *Advancing critical criminology: Theory and application*, ed. W. S. DeKeseredy and B. Perry, 199–218. Lanham, Md.: Lexington Books.

Donnermeyer, J. F., and G. H. Phillips. 1982. The nature of vandalism among rural youth. In *Rural crime: Integrating research and prevention*, ed. T. J. Carter, G. H. Phillips, J. F. Donnermeyer, and T. N. Wurschmidt. Totowa, N.J.: Allanheld, Osmun.

———. 1984. Vandals and vandalism in the rural U.S.A. In *Vandalism: Motivations and Behaviour*, ed. C. Levi-Leboyer. Amsterdam: North-Holland Press.

Dragiewicz, M., and W. S. DeKeseredy. 2008. *A needs gap assessment report on abused women without legal representation in the family courts.* Oshawa, Ont.: Luke's Place Support and Resource Centre.

Durkheim, E. 1964. *The division of labor in society.* New York: Free Press.

Dutton, D. G. 2006. *Rethinking domestic violence.* Vancouver: UBC Press.

Economic Research Council. 2004. *Rural poverty at a glance.* Washington, D.C.: ERS.

Edleson, J. L., and A. L. Bible. 2001. Collaborating for women's safety: Partnerships between research and practice. In *Sourcebook on violence against women*, ed. C. M. Renzetti, J. L. Edleson, and R. K. Bergen, 73–95. Thousand Oaks, Calif.: Sage.

Edwards, R. 2004. *Staying home, leaving domestic violence: Promoting choices for women leaving abusive partners.* Sydney: Australian Domestic and Family Violence Clearinghouse.

Ehrhart, J. K., and B. R. Sandler. 1985. *Campus gang rape: Party games?* Project on the Status and Education of Women. Washington, D.C.: Association of American Colleges.

Einstadter, W., and S. Henry. 1995. *Criminological theory: An analysis of its underlying assumptions.* New York: Harcourt Brace.

Ellen, R. F. 1984. *Ethnographic research.* New York: Academic Press.

Ellis, D., and W. S. DeKeseredy. 1997. Rethinking estrangement, interventions, and intimate femicide. *Violence against Women* 3:590–609.

Evans, C. 2002. Kids on campus weather funding cuts. *Athens News,* May 7.

Fagen, D. 2005. Perceptions of collective efficacy among abused women in rural

Appalachia. M.A. thesis, Department of Sociology and Anthropology, Ohio University.

Faludi, S. 1991. *Backlash: The undeclared war against American women.* New York: Crown.

Fassinger, P. A., and H. K. Schwartzweller. 1984. The work of farm women: A midwestern study. In *Research in rural sociology and development,* ed. H. K. Schwartzweller, 37–60. Greenwich, Conn.: JAI.

Fekete, J. 1994. *Moral panic: Biopolitics rising.* Montreal: Robert Davies.

Feldman, T. 2004. Quilts for change. *Quiltations,* September, 4.

Fenstermaker, S. 1989. Acquaintance rape on campus: Responsibility and attributions of crime. In *Violence in dating relationships: Emerging social issues,* ed. M. Pirog-Good and J. Stets, 257–271. New York: Praeger.

Ferguson, I. 1996. *A preliminary investigation into offensive and illegal content on the Internet: Deviant criminal pornography.* Ottawa: Justice Canada.

Ferrell, J. 1993. *Crimes of style: Urban graffiti and the politics of criminality.* New York: Garland.

Finkelhor, D., and K. Yllo. 1985. *License to rape: Sexual abuse of wives.* New York: Holt, Rinehart and Winston.

Fischer, C. 1995. The subcultural theory of urbanism: A twentieth-year assessment. *American Journal of Sociology* 101:543–577.

Fletcher, S., D. Lunn, and L. Reith. 1996. Fear on the farm: Rural women take action against domestic violence. *Women and Environments* 38:27–29.

Fleury, R. E., C. M. Sullivan, and D. I. Bybee. 2000. When ending the relationship does not end the violence: Women's experiences of violence by former partners. *Violence against Women* 6:1363–1383.

Ford, D. A. 2003. Coercing victim participation in domestic violence prosecutions. *Journal of Interpersonal Violence* 18:669–684.

Foster, G. S., and R. L. Hummel. 1997. Wham, bam, thank you, Sam: Critical dimensions of the persistence of hillbilly caricatures. *Sociological Spectrum* 17:157–176.

Frank, R. 2003. When bad things happen in good places: Pastoralism in big-city newspaper coverage of small-town violence. *Rural Sociology* 68:207–230.

Freudenburg, W. R. 1986. The density of acquaintanceship: An overlooked variable in community research. *American Journal of Sociology* 92:27–63.

Frieze, I. 1983. Investigating the causes and consequences of marital rape. *Signs: Journal of Women in Culture and Society* 8:532–553.

Funk, R. E. 1993. *Stopping rape: A challenge for men.* Philadelphia: New Society Publishers.

———. 2006. *Reaching men: Strategies for preventing sexist attitudes, behaviors, and violence.* Indianapolis: JIST Life.

Gagne, P. L. 1992. Appalachian women: Violence and social control. *Journal of Contemporary Ethnography* 20:387–415.

Gallup-Black, A. 2005. Twenty years of rural and urban trends in family and intimate partner homicide. *Homicide Studies* 9:149–173.

Gartner, R., M. Dawson, and M. Crawford. 2001. Women killing: Intimate femicide in Ontario, 1874–1994. In *Femicide in global perspective,* ed. D.E.H. Russell and R. A. Harmes, 147–165. New York: Teachers College Press.

Gayford, J. J. 1975. Wife battering: A preliminary survey of 100 cases. *British Medical Journal* 1:194–197.

Gelles, R. J., and M. A. Straus. 1988. *Intimate violence: The causes and consequences of abuse in the American family.* New York: Simon and Schuster.

Gelsthorpe, L., and A. Morris. 1988. Feminism and criminology in Britain. *British Journal of Criminology* 28:93–110.

Gilbert, N. 1991. The phantom epidemic of sexual assault. *Public Interest* 103:54–65.

Gilligan, J. 2001. *Preventing violence.* New York: Thames and Hudson.

Gilliom, J. 2001. *Overseers of the poor: Surveillance, resistance, and the limits of privacy.* Chicago: University of Chicago Press.

Godenzi, A., M. D. Schwartz, and W. S. DeKeseredy. 2001. Toward a gendered social bond/male peer support theory of university woman abuse. *Critical Criminology* 10:1–16.

Goeckermann, C., K. Hamberger, and K. Barber. 1994. Issues of domestic violence unique to rural areas. *Wisconsin Medical Journal* 93:473–479.

Goetting, A. 1999. *Getting out: Life stories of women who left abusive men.* New York: Columbia University Press.

Gondolf, E. W. 1999. MCMI-III results for batterer program participation in four cities: Less "pathological" than expected. *Journal of Family Violence* 14:1–17.

Grama, J. L. 2000. Women forgotten: Difficulties faced by rural victims of domestic violence. *American Journal of Family Law* 14:173–187.

Grant, J. 2006. Women and drugs: A feminist perspective. In *Advancing critical criminology: Theory and application,* ed. W. S. DeKeseredy and B. Perry, 179–198. Lanham, Md.: Lexington Books.

———. 2008. *Charting women's journeys: From addiction to recovery.* Lanham, Md.: Lexington.

Gray, D. 2007. Foreword to *Crime in rural Australia,* ed. E. Barclay, J. F. Donnermeyer, J. Scott, and R. Hogg, v–vi. Sydney, Aus.: Federation Press.

Hagan, J. 1985. The assumption of natural science methods: Criminological positivism. In *Theoretical methods in criminology,* ed. R. F. Meier, 75–92. Beverly Hills, Calif.: Sage.

Hamberger, L. 1993. Comments on Pagelow's myth of psychopathology in woman battering. *Journal of Interpersonal Violence* 8:132–136.

Hammer, R. 2002. *Antifeminism and family terrorism: A critical feminist perspective.* Lanham, Md.: Rowman and Littlefield.

Hardesty, J. L. 2002. Separation assault in the context of postdivorce parenting: An integrative review of the literature. *Violence against Women* 8:597–621.

Harmon, P. A., and J. V. P. Check. 1989. *The role of pornography in woman abuse.* Toronto: York University's LaMarsh Research Center on Violence and Conflict Resolution.

Harney, P. A., and C. L. Muehlenhard. 1991. Rape. In *Sexual coercion: A sourcebook on its nature, causes, and prevention,* ed. E. Grauerholz and M. A. Koralewski, 3–16. Lexington, Mass.: Lexington Books.

Harris, R., and R. Bologh. 1985. The dark side of love: Blue and white collar wife abuse. *Victimology* 10:242–252.

Hay, D. A., and G. S. Basran. 1992. Introduction to *Rural sociology in Canada,* ed. D. A. Hay and G. S. Basran, ix–x. Toronto: Oxford University Press.

Hazler, R. 1996. *Breaking the cycle of violence: Interventions for bullying and victimization.* Washington, D.C.: Accelerated Development.

Hey, V. 1986. *Patriarchy and pub culture.* London: Tavistock.

Hirschi, T. 1969. *Causes of delinquency.* Berkeley: University of California Press.

Hogg, R., and C. Carrington. 2003. Violence, spatiality, and other rurals. *Australian and New Zealand Journal of Criminology* 36:293–319.

———. 2006. *Policing the rural crisis.* Sydney, Aus.: Federation Press.

Holland, G. 2006. *Rural crime prevention: Vandalism.* Norman: Oklahoma State University.

Horn, P. 1992. Beating back the revolution. *Dollars and Sense,* December, 12.

Hornosty, J., and D. Doherty. 2002. Responding to wife abuse in farm and rural communities: Searching for solutions that work. SIPP Public Policy Paper No. 10. Fredericton, New Brunswick: Muriel McQueen Fergusson Centre for Family Violence Research.

Hotaling, G., and D. Sugarman. 1986. An analysis of risk markers and husband-to-wife violence: The current state of knowledge. *Violence and Victims* 1:102–124.

Huffman, T. 2005. Abuse victims need help to leave. *Toronto Star,* June 1.

Inge, T. D. 1989. Comic strips. In *Encyclopedia of southern culture,* ed. C. R. Wilson and W. Ferris, 914–915. Chapel Hill: University of North Carolina Press.

Iovanni, L., and S. L. Miller. 2001. Criminal justice responses to domestic violence: Law enforcement and the courts. In *Sourcebook on violence against women,* ed. C. M. Renzetti, J. L. Edleson, and R. K. Bergen, 303–328. Thousand Oaks, Calif.: Sage.

Ireland, T. O., T. P. Thornberry, and R. Loeber. 2003. Violence among adolescents living in public housing: A two-site analysis. *Criminology and Public Policy* 3:3–38.

Jacobs, J. 2004. *Dark age ahead.* Toronto: Vintage Canada.

Jaffe, P. G., N. K. Lemon, and S. E. Poisson. 2003. *Child custody and domestic violence: A call for safety and accountability.* Thousand Oaks, Calif.: Sage.

James, S. 1997. Crime prevention and public housing: The dynamics of control. In *Crime prevention in Australia: Issues in policy and research,* ed. P. O'Malley and A. Sutton, 38–63. Annandale, Aus.: Federation Press.

Jargowsky, P. A. 1997. *Poverty and place: Ghettos, barrios, and the American city.* New York: Russell Sage Foundation.

Jasinski, J. L. 2001. Theoretical explanations for violence against women. In *Sourcebook on violence against women,* ed. C. M. Renzetti, J. L. Edleson, and R. K. Bergen, 5–22. Thousand Oaks, Calif.: Sage.

Jensen, L. 2006. At the razor's edge: Building hope for America's rural poor. *Rural Realities* 1:1–8.

Jensen, R. 1995. Pornographic lives. *Violence against Women* 1:32–54.

———. 2007. *Getting off: Pornography and the end of masculinity.* Cambridge, Mass.: South End Press.

Jewkes, R., K. Dunkle, M. P. Koss, J. B. Levin, M. Nduna, N. Jama, and Y. Sikweyiya. 2006. Rape perpetration by young, rural South African men: Prevalence, patterns, and risk factors. *Social Science and Medicine* 63:2949–2961.

Jobes, P. C. 1997. Gender competition and the preservation of community in the allocation of administrative positions in small rural towns in Montana: A research note. *Rural Sociology* 62:315–334.

Jobes, P. C., E. Barclay, H. Weinand, and J. F. Donnermeyer. 2004. A structural analysis of social disorganization and crime in rural communities in Australia. *Australian and New Zealand Journal of Criminology* 37:114–140.

Johnson, H. 1996. *Dangerous domains: Violence against women in Canada.* Toronto: Nelson.

Johnson, H., and V. F. Sacco. 1995. Researching violence against women: Statistics Canada's national survey. *Canadian Journal of Criminology* 37:281–304.

Johnson, K. 2006. *Demographic trends in rural and small town America*. Durham: University of New Hampshire, Carsey Institute.

Johnson, M. P. 2008. *A typology of domestic violence: Intimate terrorism, violent resistance, and situational couple violence*. Boston: Northeastern University Press.

Jones, T., B. D. MacLean, and J. Young. 1986. *The Islington crime survey*. Aldershot, U.K.: Gower.

Katz, J. 2006. *The macho paradox: Why some men hurt women and how all men can help*. Naperville, Ill.: Sourcebooks.

Kimmel, M. S., and T. E. Mosmiller. 1992. Introduction to *Against the tide: Pro-feminist men in the United States, 1776–1990*, ed. M. S. Kimmel and T. E. Mosmiller, 1–46. Boston: Beacon Press.

Koss, M. P., C. A. Gidycz, and N. Wisniewski. 1987. The scope of rape: Incidence and prevalence of sexual aggression and victimization in a national sample of higher education students. *Journal of Consulting and Clinical Psychology* 55:162–170.

Krannich, R. S., and A. E. Luloff. 2002. A 50-year perspective on persistence and change: Lessons from the rural studies communities. In *Persistence and change in rural communities*, ed. A. E. Luloff and R. S. Krannich, 171–177. Wallingford, U.K.: CABI.

Krishnan, S. P., J. C. Hilbert, and M. Pase. 2001. An examination of intimate partner violence in rural communities: Results from a hospital emergency department study from Southwest United States. *Family Community Health* 24:1–14.

Kurz, D. 1995. *For richer, for poorer: Mothers confront divorce*. New York: Routledge.

Lab, S. F. 2003. Let's put it into context. *Criminology and Public Policy* 3:39–44.

———. 2007. *Crime prevention: Approaches, practices, and evaluations*. Cincinnati: Anderson.

Lasley, P., F. L. Leistritz, L. M. Lobao, and K. Meyer. 1995. *Beyond the amber waves of grain: An examination of social and economic restructuring in the heartland*. Boulder, Colo.: Westview.

LaViolette, A. D., and O. W. Barnett. 2000. *It could happen to anyone: Why battered women stay*. Thousand Oaks, Calif.: Sage.

Lawtey, A., and M. Deane. 2001. *Making rural communities safer: Consultation on community safety*. London: Nacro Crime and Social Policy Section.

Lee, M. 2008. Civic community in the hinterland: Toward a theory of rural social structure and violence. *Criminology* 46:447–478.

Lefkowitz, B. 1997. *Our guys*. New York: Vintage.

Lehman, P. 2006. Introduction: "A dirty little secret"—Why teach and study pornography? In *Pornography: Film and culture*, ed. P. Lehman, 1–24. New Brunswick, N.J.: Rutgers University Press.

LeMasters, E. E. 1975. *Blue-collar aristocrats: Life-styles at a working-class tavern*. Madison: University of Wisconsin Press.

Leukefeld, C., R. Clayton, and J. Myers. 1992. Rural drug and alcohol treatment. *Drugs and Society* 7:95–116.

Levant, R. 1994. Male violence against female partners: Roots in male socialization and development. Paper presented at the annual meeting of the American Psychological Association, Los Angeles.

Lewis, S. H. 2003. *Unspoken crimes: Sexual assault in rural America*. Enola, Pa.: National Sexual Violence Resource Center.

Lichter, S. R., D. Amundson, and L. Lichter. 2003. *Perceptions of rural America: Media coverage.* Washington, D.C.: Center for Media and Public Affairs.

Liepins, R. 2000. New energies for an old idea: Reworking approaches to "community" in contemporary rural studies. *Journal of Rural Studies* 16:23–35.

Lips, H. M. 2005. *Sex and gender: An introduction.* New York: McGraw-Hill.

Little, J. 2003. "Riding the rural love train": Heterosexuality and the rural community. *Sociologia Ruralis* 43:401–417.

Little, J., and R. Panelli. 2003. Gender research in rural geography. *Gender, Place, and Culture* 10:281–289.

Lobao, L., and K. Meyer. 2001. The great agricultural transition: Crisis, change, and social consequences of twentieth-century U.S. farming. *Annual Review of Sociology* 27:103–124.

Logan, T. K., J. Cole, L. Shannon, and R. Walker. 2006. *Partner stalking: How women respond, cope, and survive.* New York: Springer.

Logan, T. K., L. Evans, E. Stevenson, and C. E. Jordan. 2005. Barriers to services for rural and urban survivors of rape. *Journal of Interpersonal Violence* 20:591–616.

Logan, T. K., E. Stevenson, L. Evans, and C. Leukefeld. 2004. Rural and urban women's perceptions to barriers to health, mental health, and criminal justice services: Implications for victim services. *Violence and Victims* 19:37–62.

Logan, T. K., and R. Walker. 2004. Separation as a risk factor for victims of intimate partner violence: Beyond lethality and injury. *Journal of Interpersonal Violence* 19:1478–1486.

Logan, T. K., R. Walker, and C. Leukefeld. 2001. Rural, urban-influenced, and urban differences among domestic violence arrestees. *Journal of Interpersonal Violence* 16:266–283.

Luke's Place. 2007. *Proposal to conduct a needs assessment and gap analysis for abused women unrepresented in the family law system.* Oshawa, Ont.: Luke's Place.

Lynch, M. J., R. Michalowski, and W. B. Groves. 2000. *The new primer in radical criminology: Critical perspectives on crime, power, and identity.* Monsey, N.Y.: Criminal Justice Press.

MacLean, B. D. 1996. A program of local crime-survey research for Canada. In *Crime and society: Readings in critical criminology,* ed. B. D. MacLean, 73–105. Toronto: Copp Clark.

MacLeod, L. 1987. *Battered but not beaten: Preventing wife battering in Canada.* Ottawa: Canadian Advisory Council on the Status of Women.

Mahoney, M. R. 1991. Legal issues of battered women: Redefining the issue of separation. *Michigan Law Review* 90:1–94.

Mahoney, P., and L. M. Williams. 1998. Sexual assault in marriage: Prevalence, consequences, and treatment of wife rape. In *Partner violence: A comprehensive review of 20 years of research,* ed. J. L. Jasinski and L. M. Williams, 113–162. Thousand Oaks, Calif.: Sage.

Mahoney, P., L. M. Williams, and C. M. West. 2001. Violence against women by intimate relationship partners. In *Sourcebook on violence against women,* ed. C. M. Renzetti, J. L. Edleson, and R. K. Bergen, 143–178. Thousand Oaks, Calif.: Sage.

McFarlane, J., and A. Malecha. 2005. *Sexual assault among intimates: Frequency, consequences, and treatments.* Final Report, grant #2002-WG-BX-0020. Washington, D.C.: Department of Justice, National Institute of Justice.

McMurray, A. M., I. D. Froyland, D. G. Bell, and D. J. Curnow. 2000. Post-separation violence: The male perspective. *Journal of Family Studies* 6:89–105.

Messerschmidt, J. W. 1993. *Masculinities and crime: Critique and reconceptualization.* Lanham, Md.: Rowman and Littlefield.

———. 2000. *Nine lives: Adolescent masculinities, the body, and violence.* Boulder, Colo.: Westview.

Mihorean, K. 2005. Trends in self-reported spousal violence. In *Family violence in Canada: A statistical profile 2005*, ed. K. AuCoin, 13–32. Ottawa: Statistics Canada.

Miller, B. A., and W. R. Downs. 1993. The impact of family violence on the use of alcohol by women. *Alcohol Health and Research World* 17:137–143.

Miller, J., and M. D. Schwartz. 1992. Lewd lighters and dick-ee darts: The commodification of women through sexual objects. Paper presented at the annual meeting of the American Society of Criminology, New Orleans.

Miller, K. 2007. Traversing the spatial divide: Gender, place, and delinquency. *Feminist Criminology* 2:202–222.

Miller, T. W., and L. J. Veltkamp. 1989. Child sexual abuse: The abusing family in rural America. *International Journal of Family Psychiatry* 9:259–275.

Navin, S., R. Stockum, and J. Campbell-Ruggaard. 1993. Battered women in rural America. *Journal of Human Educational Development* 32:9–16.

Newman, O. 1972. *Defensible space: Crime prevention through urban design.* New York: Macmillan.

Niehaus, I. 2005. Masculine dominance in sexual violence: Interpreting accounts of three cases of rape in the South African Lowveld. In *Men behaving differently*, ed. G. Reid and L. Walker. Cape Town: Juta.

Oetting, E. R., and J. F. Donnermeyer. 1998. Primary socialization theory: The etiology of drug use and deviance. *Substance Use and Misuse* 33:995–1206.

O'Leary, D. 1993. Through a psychological lens: Personality traits, personality disorders, and levels of violence. In *Current controversies on family violence*, ed. R. J. Gelles and D. R. Loseke, 7–30. Thousand Oaks, Calif.: Sage.

Oliver, P. 2006. Review of the film *Country.* Jessica Lang tribute site, *http://home.hiwaay.nt/~oliver/jlcountry.htm.*

Osgood, D. W., and J. M. Chambers. 2000. Social disorganization outside the metropolis: An analysis of rural youth violence. *Criminology* 38:81–115.

———. 2003. *Community correlates of rural youth violence.* Washington, D.C.: U.S. Department of Justice.

Pagelow, M. D. 1992. Adult victims of domestic violence: Battered women. *Journal of Interpersonal Violence* 7:87–120.

———. 1993. Response to Hamberger's comments. *Journal of Interpersonal Violence* 8:137–139.

Pateman, C. 1988. *The sexual contract.* London: Polity.

Polk, K. 1994. *When men kill: Scenarios of masculine violence.* Cambridge: Cambridge University Press.

———. 2003. Masculinities, femininities, and homicide: Competing explanations for male violence. In *Controversies in critical criminology*, ed. M. D. Schwartz and S. E. Hatty, 133–146. Cincinnati: Anderson.

Polk, K., and D. Ranson. 1991. The role of gender in intimate violence. *Australia and New Zealand Journal of Criminology* 24:15–24.

Porter, T. 2006a. Becoming part of the solution: A Call to Men: National Association of Men and Women Committed to Ending Violence against Women. www.acalltomen.com/page.php?id=53.

———. 2006b. *Well meaning men: Breaking out of the man box.* Charlotte, N.C.: A

Call to Men: National Association of Men and Women Committed to Ending Violence against Women.

Price, R. 2002. Cheaper labor moves Rocky Shoe production to Puerto Rico. *Puerto Rico Herald.* May 10.

Ptacek, J. 1999. *Battered women in the courtroom: The power of judicial responses.* Boston: Northeastern University Press.

Purdon, C. 2003. *Woman abuse and Ontario Works in a rural community: Rural women speak out about their experiences with Ontario Works.* Ottawa: Status of Women Canada.

Raine, P. 2001. *Women's perspectives on drugs and alcohol: The vicious circle.* Hampshire, U.K.: Ashgate.

Random House. 2003. *Our Guys* reading group center, *www.randomhouse.com/vintage/read/ourguys/.*

Rapaport, E. 1994. The death penalty and the domestic discount. In *The public nature of private violence,* ed. M. Fineman and R. Mykitiuk, 224–254. New York: Routledge.

Raphael, J. 2001. Public housing and domestic violence. *Violence against Women* 7: 699–706.

Renzetti, C. M. 1997. Confessions of a reformed positivist: Feminist participatory research as good social science. In *Researching sexual violence: Methodological and personal perspectives,* ed. M. D. Schwartz, 131–143. Thousand Oaks, Calif.: Sage.

Renzetti, C. M., and D. J. Curran. 2002. *Women, men, and society.* Boston: Allyn and Bacon.

Renzetti, C. M., and S. L. Maier. 2002. "Private" crime in public housing: Fear of crime and violent victimization among women public housing residents. *Women's Health and Urban Life* 1:46–65.

Ritzer, G. 2008. *The McDonaldization of society.* Thousand Oaks, Calif.: Pine Forge Press.

Rodgers, K. 1994. *Wife assault: The findings of a national survey.* Ottawa: Canadian Centre for Justice Statistics.

Rogers, E., R. Burdge, P. Korsching, and J. F. Donnermeyer. 1988. *Social change in rural societies.* Englewood Cliffs, N.J.: Prentice-Hall.

Rogness, M. 2003. Toward an integrated male peer support model of marital/cohabitation rape in the United States. M.A. thesis, Department of Sociology and Anthropology, Ohio University.

Roiphe, K. 1993. *The morning after: Sex, fear, and feminism on campus.* Boston: Little, Brown.

Rothman, E. F., D. Hemenway, M. Miller, and D. Azrael. 2005. Batterers' use of guns to threaten intimate partners. *Journal of the American Medical Women's Association* 60:62–80.

Rubak, B., and K. S. Menard. 2001. Rural-urban differences in sexual victimization and reporting: Analyses using UCR and crisis center data. *Criminal Justice and Behavior* 28:131–155.

Rudy, E. B., P. J. Estok, M. E. Kerr, and L. Menzel. 1994. Research incentives: Money versus gifts. *Nursing Research* 43:253–255.

Russell, D.E.H. 1990. *Rape in marriage.* New York: Macmillan.

———. 1998. *Dangerous relationships: Pornography, misogyny, and rape.* Thousand Oaks, Calif.: Sage.

———. 2001. Femicide: Some men's "final solution" for women. In *Femicide in global perspective*, ed. D.E.H. Russell and R. A. Harmes, 176–188. New York: Teacher's College Press.

Ryan, V., and J. Popour. 1983. *Five-year women's plan developed by the capital area substance abuse commission for the office of substance abuse*. Washington, D.C.: Department of Health.

Sampson, R. J., and W. B. Groves. 1989. Community structure and crime: Testing social disorganization theory. *American Journal of Sociology* 94:774–802.

Sampson, R. J., S. W. Raudenbush, and F. Earls. 1997. Neighborhoods and violent crime: A multilevel study of collective efficacy. *Science* 277:918–924.

———. 1998. *Neighborhood collective efficacy: Does it help reduce violence?* Washington, D.C.: U.S. Department of Justice.

Sanday, P. R. 1990. *Fraternity gang rape*. New York: New York University Press.

Saville, G. 2004. Editor's introduction. *CPTED Journal* 3:1–2.

Saville, G., and T. Clear. 2000. Community renaissance with community justice. *Neighborworks Journal* 18:19–24.

Saville, G., and G. Cleveland. 1997. Second generation CPTED: An antidote to the social Y2K virus of urban design. Paper presented at the Second Annual International CPTED Conference, Orlando, December.

Schechter, S. 1988. Building bridges between activists, professionals, and researchers. In *Feminist perspectives on wife abuse*, ed. K. Yllo and M. Bograd, 299–312. Beverly Hills, Calif.: Sage.

Schur, E. 1984. *Labeling women deviant: Gender, stigma, and social control*. Philadelphia: Temple University Press.

Schwartz, M. D. 1988. Marital status and woman abuse theory. *Journal of Family Violence* 3:239–248.

———. 1989. Asking the right questions: Battered wives are not all passive. *Sociological Viewpoints* 5:46–61.

———. 2000. Methodological issues in the use of survey data for measuring and characterizing violence against women. *Violence against Women* 6: 815–838.

Schwartz, M. D., and W. S. DeKeseredy. 1997. *Sexual assault on the college campus: The role of male peer support*. Thousand Oaks, Calif.: Sage.

———. 1998. Pornography and the abuse of Canadian women in dating relationships. *Humanity and Society* 22:137–154.

Schwartz, M. D., W. S. DeKeseredy, D. Tait, and S. Alvi. 2001. Male peer support and a feminist routine activities theory: Understanding sexual assault on the college campus. *Justice Quarterly* 18:623–649.

Schwartz, M. D., and S. E. Hatty, eds. 2003. *Controversies in critical criminology*. Cincinnati: Anderson.

Schwartz, M. D., and M. S. Leggett. 1999. Bad dates or emotional trauma? The aftermath of campus sexual assault. *Violence against Women* 5:251–271.

Scott, J., R. Hogg, E. Barclay, and J. F. Donnermeyer. 2007. There's crime out there, but not as we know it: Rural criminology—the last frontier. In *Crime in rural Australia*, ed. E. Barclay, J. F. Donnermeyer, J. Scott, and R. Hogg, 1–12. Sydney, Aus.: Federation Press.

Scully, D. 1990. *Understanding sexual violence: A study of convicted rapists*. Boston: Unwin Hyman.

Sernau, S. 2006. *Global problems: The search for equity, peace, and sustainability*. Boston: Pearson.

Serran, G., and P. Firestone. 2004. Intimate partner homicide: A review of the male proprietariness and the self-defence theories. *Journal of Aggression and Violent Behavior* 9:1–15.

Sev'er, A. 1997. Recent or imminent separation and intimate violence against women: A conceptual overview and some Canadian examples. *Violence against Women* 3: 566–589.

———. 2001. *An ode to survivors of abuse.* Toronto: Department of Sociology, University of Toronto.

———. 2002. *Fleeing the house of horrors: Women who have left abusive partners.* Toronto: University of Toronto Press.

Sharps, P. W., J. C. Campbell, D. W. Campbell, F. Gary, and D. Webster. 2001. The role of alcohol use in intimate partner femicide. *Journal on Addictions* 10:1–14.

———. 2003. Risky mix: Drinking, drug use, and homicide. *NIJ Journal* 250:8–13.

Sherman, J. 2005. *Men without sawmills: Masculinity, rural poverty, and family stability.* Columbia, Mo.: Rural Poverty Research Center.

Simon, S. 2004. Hard-core porn hits the heartland: Rural superstores are "doing great." *Concord Monitor,* December 7. *www.cmonitor.com/apps/pbcs.dll/article? AID=/20041207/REPOSITORY/412070332/1014.*

Sinclair, R. L. 2002. Male peer support and male-to-female dating abuse committed by socially displaced male youth: An exploratory study. PhD dissertation, Department of Sociology and Anthropology, Carleton University.

Skinner, T., M. Hester, and E. Malos. 2005. Methodology, feminism, and gender violence. In *Researching gender violence: Feminist methodology in action,* ed. T. Skinner, M. Hester, and E. Malos, 1–22. Portland, Ore.: Willan.

Smith, M. D. 1990. Patriarchal ideology and wife beating: A test of a feminist hypothesis. *Violence and Victims* 5:257–273.

———. 1994. Enhancing the quality of survey data on violence against women: A feminist approach. *Gender and Society* 18:109–127.

Sokoloff, N. J., ed. 2005. *Domestic violence at the margins: Readings on race, class, gender, and culture.* New Brunswick, N.J.: Rutgers University Press.

Sokoloff, N. J., and I. Dupont. 2005. Domestic violence: Examining the intersections of race, class, and gender—An introduction. In *Domestic violence at the margins: Readings on race, class, gender, and culture,* ed. N. J. Sokoloff, 1–14. New Brunswick, N.J.: Rutgers University Press.

Stanko, E. A. 1997. Should I stay or should I go? Some thoughts on variants of intimate violence. *Violence against Women* 3:629–635.

———. 2006. Theorizing about violence: Observations from the Economic and Social Research Council's Violence Research Program. *Violence against Women* 12:543–555.

Stark, E. 1993. Mandatory arrest of batterers: A reply to its critics. *American Behavioral Scientist* 36:651–680.

———. 2007. *Coercive control: How men entrap women in personal life.* New York: Oxford University Press.

Statistics Canada. 2005. Study: Social relationships in rural and urban Canada. *Daily,* June 21.

Stein, D. 1999. New TANF flexibility gives states greater opportunity to support working families. *Alternatives* 7:1–2.

Stone, K. E. 1997. *Impact of the Wal-Mart phenomenon on rural communities.* Proceedings of the National Public Policy Education Conference. Charleston, S.C., October.

Stout, K. D. 2001. Intimate femicide: A national demographic overview. In *Femicide in global perspective*, ed. D.E.H. Russell and R. A. Harmes, 41–49. New York: Teacher's College Press.

Straus, M.A. 1979. Measuring intrafamily conflict and violence: The Conflict Tactics (CT) Scales. *Journal of Marriage and the Family* 41:75–88.

———. 1983. Ordinary violence, child abuse, and wife beating: What do they have in common? In *The dark side of families: Current family violence research*, ed. D. Finkelhor, R. J. Gelles, G. Hotaling, and M. A. Straus, 213–234. Beverly Hills, Calif.: Sage.

Straus, M. A., R. J. Gelles, and S. Steinmetz. 1981. *Behind closed doors: Violence in the American family*. Newbury Park, Calif.: Sage.

Straus, M.A., S. L. Hamby, S. Boney-McCoy, and D. B. Sugarman. 1996. The revised Conflict Tactics Scales (Conn.S2): Development and preliminary psychometric data. *Journal of Family Issues* 17:283–316.

Taylor, R. B. 2001. The ecology of crime, fear, and delinquency: Social disorganization versus social efficacy. In *Explaining criminals and crime*, ed. R. Paternoster and R. Bachman, 124–139. Los Angeles: Roxbury.

Thorne-Finch, R. 1992. *Ending the silence: The origins and treatment of violence against women*. Toronto: University of Toronto Press.

Tjaden, P., and N. Thonnes. 2000. *Extent, nature, and consequences of intimate partner violence: Findings from the National Violence against Women Survey*. Washington, D.C.: U.S. Department of Justice.

Tonnies, F. 1940. *Fundamental principles of sociology (gemeinschaft and gesellschaft)*. New York: American Books.

Toughill, K. 2007. StatsCan confirms: Small-town folks nicer. *Toronto Star,* June 9.

Tunnell, K. D. 2006. Socially disorganized rural communities. *Crime, Media, Culture* 2:332–337.

Turcotte, M. 2005. *Social engagement and civic participation: Are rural and small town populations really at an advantage?* Ottawa: Statistics Canada.

Tutty, L. M. 2006. *Effective practices in sheltering women leaving violence in intimate relationships*. Toronto: YWCA Canada.

U.S. Bureau of Justice Statistics. 2007. *Intimate partner violence in the US: Victim characteristics*. Washington, D.C.: U.S. Department of Justice.

Vallee, B. 2007. *The war on women*. Toronto: Key Porter.

Venkatesh, S. A. 2000. *American project: The rise and fall of a modern ghetto*. Cambridge, Mass.: Harvard University Press.

———. 2006. *Off the books: The underground economy of the urban poor*. Cambridge, Mass.: Harvard University Press.

Victoria Women's Sexual Assault Centre. 1994. *Today's Talk about Sexual Assault*. Victoria, B.C.: Victoria Women's Sexual Assault Centre.

Vigdor, E. R., and J. A. Mercy. 2006. Do laws restricting access to firearms by domestic violence offenders prevent intimate partner homicide? *Evaluation Review: A Journal of Applied Social Research* 30:313–346.

Wacquant, L.J.D. 1997. Three pernicious premises in the study of the American ghetto. *International Journal of Urban and Regional Research,* July, 341–353.

Walker, R., T. K. Logan, C. E. Jordan, and J. C. Campbell. 2004. An integrative review of separation in the context of victimization: Consequences and implications for women. *Trauma, Violence, and Abuse* 5:143–193.

Walker, S. 1998. *Sense and nonsense about crime and drugs: A policy guide*. Belmont, Calif.: West/Wadsworth.

Ward, C. A. 1995. *Attitudes toward rape: Feminist and social psychological perspectives*. Thousand Oaks, Calif.: Sage.

Warr, M. 2002. *Companions in crime: The social aspects of criminal conduct.* Cambridge: Cambridge University Press.

Websdale, N. 1995. An ethnographic assessment of policing of domestic violence in rural eastern Kentucky. *Social Justice* 22:102–122.

———. 1998. *Rural woman battering and the justice system: An ethnography.* Thousand Oaks, Calif.: Sage.

———. 2001. Men researching violence against women. In *Sourcebook on violence against women*, ed. C. M. Renzetti, J. L. Edleson, and R. K. Bergen, 53–56. Thousand Oaks, Calif.: Sage.

Websdale, N., and B. Johnson. 2005. Reducing woman battering: The role of structural approaches. In *Domestic violence at the margins: Readings on race, class, gender, and culture*, ed. N. J. Sokoloff, 389–415. New Brunswick, N.J.: Rutgers University Press.

Weisheit, R. A., D. N. Falcone, and L. E. Wells. 1994. *Rural crime and rural policing.* Washington, D.C.: National Institute of Justice Research in Action Report.

———. 2006. *Crime and policing in rural and small-town America.* Long Grove, Ill.: Waveland.

Weisheit, R. A., and S. T. Kernes. 2003. Future challenges: The urbanization of rural America. In *Community policing in a rural setting*, ed. Q. C. Thurman and E. F. McGarrell, 137–147. Cincinnati: Anderson.

West, C., and D. Zimmerman. 1987. Doing gender. *Gender and Society* 1:125–151.

Whitehead, A. 1976. Sexual antagonisms in Herefordshire. In *Dependence and exploitation in work and marriage*, ed. D. Barker and S. Allen, 169–203. London: Longman.

Williams, L. 1999. *Hard core: Power, pleasure, and the "frenzy of the visible."* Berkeley: University of California Press.

Williamson, J. W. 1995. *Hillbillyland: What the movies did to the mountains and what the mountains did to the movies.* Chapel Hill: University of North Carolina Press.

Wilson, M., and M. Daly. 1992. Till death do us part. In *Femicide: The politics of woman killing*, ed. J. Radford and D.E.H. Russell, 83–98. New York: Twayne.

———. 1994. *Spousal homicide.* Ottawa: Canadian Centre for Justice Statistics.

Wilson, W. J. 1996. *When work disappears: The world of the new urban poor.* New York: Knopf.

Wineman, N. M., and E. Durand. 1992. Incentives and rewards for subjects in nursing research. *Western Journal of Nursing Research* 14:526–531.

Wojcicki, J. 2002. "She drank his money": Survival sex and the problem of violence in taverns in Gauteng province, South Africa. *Medical Anthropology* 16:267–293.

Wood, K. 2005. Contextualizing group rape in post-apartheid South Africa. *Culture, Health, and Sexuality* 7:303–317.

Wood, K., and R. Jewkes. 2001. "Dangerous" love: Reflections on violence among Xhosa township youth. In *Changing men in South Africa*, ed. R. Morrell, 78–98. Pietermaritzburg, South Africa: University of Natal Press.

Young, J. 1988. Radical criminology in Britain: The emergence of a competing paradigm. *British Journal of Criminology* 28:159–183.

Zerbisias, A. 2008. Packaging abuse of women as entertainment for adults: Cruel, degrading scenes "normalized" for generation brought up in dot-com world. *Toronto Star*, January 26.

Zorza, J. 2002. Domestic violence in rural America. In *Violence against women: Law, prevention, protection, enforcement, treatment, and health*, ed. J. Zorza, 14-1–14-2. Kingston, N.J.: Civic Research Institute.

Index

abuse, vii, ix, xi, 5, 12, 17, 21, 26, 33, 34, 37, 40, 44, 45, 48, 49, 61, 62, 63, 64, 66, 67, 73, 75, 79, 82, 84, 86, 90, 93, 94, 101, 105, 106, 117, 118, 138n5, 141n3; consequences of, 81, 82; male-to-female, 5; separation and divorce, 26, 40; sexual, 22, 25, 81, 88, 93, 105, 140n1; of women, 23, 35, 36. *See also* assault; battered women; separation and divorce sexual assault; woman abuse

alcohol, 64, 67, 68, 69, 70, 74, 79, 84, 86, 97, 140n3. *See also* drinking

antifeminist scholars, 32

Appalachia, 7, 8, 51, 52, 53, 112, 141n8; Ohio, 52–53, 54; women in, 13, 49

Appalachian Regional Commission (ARC), 52, 53

assault, 6, 16, 18, 33, 35, 41, 66, 86, 97, 140n13; physical, 22; sexual, xv, 3, 8, 14, 15, 17, 22, 23, 24, 25, 26, 28, 33, 41, 43, 44, 45, 46, 54, 58, 62, 63, 65, 66, 79, 82, 84, 86, 88, 89, 98, 103, 104, 108, 111, 114, 120, 122, 139n11; separation and divorce, 16, 26. *See also* separation and divorce sexual assault; sexual assault on college campus

Athens County Coalition Against Sexual Assault, xiii, 55

Australia, 13, 97, 120

Barak, G., 5–6

Barclay, E., 6, 14, 29, 124

battered women, 3, 4, 5–6, 9, 15, 17, 26, 31, 53, 93, 98, 108, 137n6; rural, 113; syndrome, 5; urban, 108. *See also* woman battering

battered women's shelter, 87; staff, 54

Block, C. R., 28

California Coalition Against Sexual Assault (CALCASA), 55

Canada, 13, 15, 16, 32, 33, 40, 76, 111, 112, 122, 139n8

Canada's Violence Against Women Survey, 16

Carrington, K., 98, 99

Chicago Women's Health Risk Survey, 15–16, 28

child, 50; care, 113, 117; custody, 5. *See also* children

children, 3, 4, 21, 39, 40, 59, 62, 64, 71, 90, 100, 106, 108, 109, 125. *See also* child

cocaine, 78. *See also* drug use; drugs

collective efficacy, viii, 9, 10, 19, 20, 88, 91, 92, 95, 115, 116–117, 120; theory, 98

community: backlash, 11; culture, 116

Conflicts Tactics Scale (CTS), 32, 138n9; CTS2, 138n9

crime, viii, ix, 2, 9, 10, 12, 13, 14, 15, 19, 20, 29, 34, 41, 48, 50, 54, 60, 68, 97, 98, 109, 111, 115, 120, 137n2, 142n8; prevention, 112

Crime Prevention Through Environmental Design (CPTED), xv, 115, 119, 121, 124

criminal justice, 54, 68, 93; officials, 15, 49, 86, 108; system, 25, 68, 92, 94, 95, 106, 109, 111, 119

criminology, viii, 6, 8, 19, 26, 31, 51, 137n4, 139n1; critical, vii, 28–29; cultural, 29; feminist, vii; rural, vii, x, xiv, 137n4

critical criminological thought, 28–29

Currie, E., 111, 115

cyberporn, 42–43. *See also* pornography

cyberspace, 42

DeKeseredy, W., vii, viii, ix, xi–xii, xiii, xv, 2, 19, 28, 30, 43, 51, 55, 56, 57–58, 60, 72, 99, 124

domestic violence, 4, 6, 53, 54, 82, 90, 96, 103, 105, 107, 108; laws, 111; scholars, 21. *See also* violence; violence against women; woman abuse

Donnermeyer, J. F., x, xiv, xi, 6, 19, 29, 99, 116, 124

drinking, 63, 67, 74, 78, 80, 87, 97, 100, 101, 113, 141n8. *See also* alcohol

drug use, 4, 48, 78, 80; illegal, 75, 141n8. *See also* cocaine; drugs; heroin

drugs, 68, 75, 78, 79, 84, 86, 106, 113, 121. *See also* cocaine; drug use; heroin

Dutton, D., 32, 36

education, 20, 59, 87, 95, 102–103, 104, 112, 113, 125; sex, 77

emotional: abuse, 40, 107; separation, 22

England, 42

Fagen, D., 11, 56

femicide, 15, 16; intimate, 137n7, 140n3, 141n7

feminism, 29

feminist, 2, 4, 30, 33, 59, 73; man, 48, 139n2; research, 47, 48; scholars, 29, 47; studies, viii

Ferguson, I., 42–43

financial outcomes, 87–88

firearms. *See* guns

Funk, R., 73

Gagne, P. L., 13

gemeinschaft, viii, 19, 137n8

gender, 8, 12, 14, 29, 32, 33, 45, 58, 71, 100, 103, 107, 117, 122, 125, 138n4, 138n7; roles, 87

Gidycz, C. A., 24

Glen Ridge, N.J., 34

good ol' boy network, 13, 49, 93, 107–108

guns, 75, 79, 80, 106, 141n7

heroin, 78; *See also* drug use; drugs

Hogg, R., 97, 98, 99

Holland, G., 121

homicide, 26, 30, 33, 41, 87, 90, 125. *See also* murder

implications, 26

informational support, 67

interviews, 48, 55, 58, 59; face-to-face, 56, 58

intimate: partner, 3, 4, 14, 15, 31, 33, 38, 44, 69; relationship, xii, 4, 9, 32, 35, 43, 79, 85, 138n5, 138n6; terrorists, 2; violence, 4, 35, 63, 138n9

Jargowsky, P., 124
Jobes, P. C., 6, 14, 124

Koss, M. P., 24

Lab, S., 51
left realism, 28
Lewis, S. H., 114, 124, 137n1
Luke's Place, 40

male: domination, 35; proprietariness, 31, 38, 39, 40, 41. *See also* male peer support
male peer support, xi–xii, xv, 20, 25, 26, 30, 41, 43, 45, 66, 68, 70, 73, 79, 97, 99, 101, 138n10, 139n13, 139n15, 139n16; model, xv, 30; research, 43, 46; theory, 49, 99; theory of separation and divorce sexual assault, 30, 99. *See also* male; patriarchal: male peer support
male-to-female violence, 3, 4, 8, 32, 122; physical, 78; rural, 9
man, well-meaning, 118–119
masculinity, 13, 33, 37, 41, 44, 67, 99, 100, 101; feminist, 116; hegemonic, 42, 97, 118; profeminist, 117. *See also* men: profeminist
media, 6, 12, 24, 25, 35, 73, 76, 77; mass, 6, 7; sexually explicit, 76–77. *See also* pornography
men: African American, 42; profeminist, 118–119, 123. *See also* masculinity
murder, 43. *See also* homicide

National Institute of Justice, xi, xiii
National Organization of Men Against Sexism (NOMAS), 118
nonintervention norms, 11, 91

Ohio Coalition Against Sexual Assault, xiii, 5
Ohio Domestic Violence Network, 55, 56, 120
Ohio University, xiii, xiv, 51, 52, 56–57, 59, 117
ol' boys network. *See* good ol' boy network

patriarchal, 11, 35, 49, 72, 67, 68, 93, 96; abusive men, xi, 44; baggage, 118; control, 22, 26, 71, 73, 97, 118; country, 37; discourses and practices, 38; dominance, 30, 40; domination, 101, 118; ideology, 54, 99; male peer support, 25, 30, 31, 41, 44; masculinity, 44, 101; men, 41; norms, 119; oppression, 95; relations, 13, 29; society, 38; subcultures, 79; terrorism, 113. *See also* masculinity; patriarchy
patriarchy, 20, 30, 38, 73, 119; familial, xii, 30, 35, 45, 72–73, 100; rural, 10, 14, 116, 119, 125; societal, 30, 31–32, 35. *See also* masculinity; patriarchal
physical health outcomes, 84
policy, xii, 4, 25, 82, 96, 99, 111, 112; analysts, 115; decisions, 5; implications, 26; makers, 113, 124; recommendations, xii, 95, 101–102, 110
pornography, xii, 26, 35, 36, 37, 45, 65, 73, 74–75, 76–77, 79, 119, 140n5. *See also* media
Porter, T., 118
positivism, 138n1
poverty, 50, 52, 60, 87, 88, 114, 115; rate, 52. *See also* unemployment
pro-abuse: male peer support, 90; male social network, 25

psychological consequences, 83–84
Purdon, C., 112–113

rape, 2, 3, 5, 13, 17, 18, 23, 25, 27, 28,
  30, 34, 35, 42, 44, 45, 62, 64, 68, 69,
  85, 88, 89, 94, 97, 101, 107, 110,
  117, 137n10; attempted, 25; and
  battering, 30, 78, 84–86; blackmail,
  62; culture, 35; date, 67; gang, 34,
  68, 69, 70, 71, 138n10; marital, 14,
  17, 20, 28, 30, 58, 92, 93; risk
  factors, 30; spousal, 17; wife, 27, 78,
  93, 114
rape crisis center, 81, 114
Renzetti, C., xv, 41, 139n1
research, xi, xiii, xiv, viii, 14, 26, 33,
  36, 43, 46, 51, 54, 55, 60, 62, 73, 79,
  96, 97, 98, 112, 137n2; assistants, 48,
  57, 59; methods, 47; rural, 6, 14,
  28–29, 124; team, 55, 59; urban, 26
risk factors, xi, 30, 61, 97
Rogness, M., 30, 99
rural: areas, 7, 9, 13, 14, 20, 80, 81, 88,
  89, 91, 95, 108, 120, 137n2, 141n1;
  communities, vii, viii, ix, xi, xv, 6, 8,
  9, 12, 13, 15, 18, 19, 20, 35, 46, 75,
  87, 94, 95, 96, 98, 99, 100, 111, 112,
  114, 115–116, 117, 120, 122,
  140n15; crime, vii, ix, 6, 20, 101,
  124, 137n4; criminologist, 14;
  culture, 80; definition of, 18–19;
  life, 7–8; Ohio, xi, 14, 30, 33, 49,
  54; Ohio women, xiii, 26, 50, 59,
  82; patriarchal relations, 13; realities,
  141n2; shelter workers, 57; shelters,
  48; sociologists, viii; sociology, vii,
  viii, xiv; U.S. communities, 25, 53,
  124; youth, 77. *See also* research
rural-urban, viii, ix, 19

Sanday, P. R., 68, 69
Schwartz, M. D., vii, viii, ix, xi, xv, 43,
  72, 99, 124

separation and divorce, xi, 15, 22, 27,
  28, 41, 43, 44, 45, 50, 54, 55, 114,
  140n1; conceptualization of, 20–21.
  See also separation and divorce
  sexual assault
separation and divorce sexual assault,
  vii, xi, xii, xv, 12, 17, 18, 27, 28,
  29–31, 35, 41, 45, 46, 49, 50, 54, 60,
  62, 64, 65, 67–68, 73, 74, 78, 79, 81,
  82, 88, 89, 92, 93, 95–99, 101, 104,
  105, 111, 113, 114, 115, 119, 124,
  138n1; in rural Ohio, xv. *See also*
  survivors; survivors, rural, of
  separation and divorce sexual
  assault
services, support, 91, 94, 112
Sev'er, A., 39
sex, 27, 29, 33, 42, 44, 61, 63, 64, 69,
  70, 73, 77, 78, 79, 83–84, 86, 103,
  108, 122, 123, 137n9, 137n10;
  forced, 22, 28, 90; play, 24; unwanted, 2, 23–24, 88, 89, 93, 107
sexual abuse: of women, 79; of poor
  and minority women, 26
sexual assault on college campus, 2,
  140n4. *See also* assault
sexual coercion, 24–25
sexual contact, 24
sexual experiences, unwanted, 57,
  58
sexual exploitation of women, 42
sexual objectification of women, 42
social: change, viii; cohesion,
  121–122; control, xii, 38, 49, 88, 92,
  93, 95, 98, 120, 121; disorganization
  theory, vii, 9, 10, 20, 98; organization, 35; programs, 115. *See also*
  collective efficacy; social support;
  theory
social support, 11, 12, 26, 87, 92, 93,
  94, 100, 102, 108; experiences,
  81–82, 92; resources, 95; services,
  58, 81, 88

Status of Women Canada (SWC), 36

survivors, 33, 49, 58, 66, 82, 83, 92, 93, 95, 96, 102, 105, 108, 109, 111, 125; abuse, xiv; advocates, 54; sexual assault, 9; wife rape, 27, 38, 78

survivors, rural, of separation and divorce sexual assault, ix, 74, 81, 92, 112. *See also* survivors

theory, xi, 96, 98, 99, 101; integrated, 30. *See also* collective efficacy; male peer support: theory; social: disorganization theory

unemployment, 87, 88, 101, 115; insurance, 113; rate, 52. *See also* poverty

United States (US), 1, 2, 4, 5, 12, 15, 16, 20, 32, 33, 35, 36, 37, 42, 47, 53, 56, 73, 75, 93, 97, 111, 113, 114, 122, 137n1, 137n4, 137n6; community, 2

US National Crime Victimization Survey, 16

US National Family Violence Survey, 61

US National Violence Against Women Survey (NAWS), 28, 140n1

urban: areas, xi; communities, 9, 14, 91, 99, 115; crime, 6

Vallee, B., 3

victim support, 12, 54

victims, ix, 1, 2, 11, 40, 43, 50, 69, 80, 81, 105, 108, 138n8; of abuse, 109; crime, vii; rape, 28

victimization, 11, 12, 26, 78, 89, 101, 103, 106; female, 99; male-to-female, 15, 61, 92, 101, 114; sexual, 2; of women, xi, 20

Victims of Crime, 102, 114

Victoria Women's Sexual Assault Center (VWSAC), 122–123

violence, vii, ix, 4, 13, 16, 17, 21, 22, 26, 30, 32, 33, 38, 41, 46, 55, 88, 96, 97, 106, 116, 123, 138n9; criminal, 111; gendered, 29, 118; on college campuses, 25; rates, 22; sexual, 14, 15, 26, 84; symmetry of, 32–33. *See also* abuse; assault

violence against women, xii, xv, 4, 10, 17, 46, 47, 48, 73, 97, 115, 116, 119, 138n7, 138n11, 141n2

Violence Against Women Act, 4

Wal-Mart, 53

war on women, 3, 26

Websdale, N., 10, 13, 19, 25, 49, 80, 98, 111, 125

wife beating, 5, 44, 60, 67, 92, 101. *See also* domestic violence

Wilson, W., 42

Wisniewski, N., 24

woman abuse, xi–xii, xiii, xv, 2, 4, 5, 8, 11, 12, 15, 20, 29, 30–31, 32, 40, 41, 43, 44, 46, 49, 55, 56, 59, 66, 67, 73, 74, 75, 78, 79, 82, 90, 92, 94, 98, 99, 102, 111, 112, 113, 114, 115, 117, 118, 119, 124, 138n11, 139n2, 139n13, 140n11; in rural communities, 121–122; research, 29; rural, 101, 139n5. *See also* abuse; assault

woman battering, 125. *See also* abuse; assault; battered women; domestic violence; wife beating

women, rural, vii, 7, 8, 26, 48–49, 50, 56, 61, 87, 88, 117, 125; victimization of, 5. *See also* rural

women, separated and divorced, 16, 17, 26; separated/divorced rural, 25. *See also* separation and divorce sexual assault

About the Authors

Walter S. DeKeseredy is a full professor at the University of Ontario Institute of Technology. He has published extensively on the topic of violence against women and has received major awards for his work from two divisions of the American Society of Criminology and two Canadian universities.

Martin D. Schwartz is a full professor at Ohio University. He is an award-winning scholar who has made numerous contributions to a rich sociological understanding of gender-related violence. He is the coauthor (with Walter DeKeseredy) of *Sexual Assault on the College Campus: The Role of Male Peer Support* (1997).